UnSelling.

The New Customer Experience

SCOTT STRATTEN

ALISON KRAMER

WILEY

For general information about our other products and services, please contact our Customer
Care Department within the United States at (800) 762-2974, outside the United States at
(317) 572-3993 or fax (317) 572-4002.

Wiley publishes in a variety of print and electronic formats and by print-on-demand. Some
material included with standard print versions of this book may not be included in e-books or in
print-on-demand. If this book refers to media such as a CD or DVD that is not included in the
version you purchased, you may download this material at http://booksupport.wiley.com. For more
information about Wiley products, visit www.wiley.com.

ISBN: 978-1-118-94300-7 (cloth)
ISBN: 978-1-118-94301-4 (ebk)
ISBN: 978-1-118-94302-1 (ebk)

Printed in the United States of America

10 9 8 7 6 5 4 3 2 1

Contents

1

UnSelling

W HEN THE WIFE of a major online company Chief Executive Officer (CEO) commits fraud at the Boston Marathon, it matters. When your latte is cold, when the head of your favorite clothing company is a racist, when a major airline sends an angry customer a reply that includes a pornographic picture, it matters. I don't want to live in a world where it doesn't.

Sales are affected. Human Resources suffers. And customers change their purchasing decisions—most long before you'd ever even considered them a prospect.

Sixty percent of all purchase decisions are now being made before you ever get a chance to share your pitch.[1] For too long in business, it's been buy or good-bye, and we've focused all our energy on the moment of the sale. Counting our sales numbers as successes and then sending customers on with too little support and products we simply shipped without care or concern for the next step. All our eyes and attention have been on our sales funnel, ignoring those outside it—both before and after the connection was all about us. We've had funnel vision for far too long, and it needs to stop.

---

[1]http://bit.ly/UnFunnelVision

UnSelling is about everything but the sell. We put all of our focus on the individual purchase transaction, while putting the rest of our business actions second. We've become blind to customer service, support, branding, experiences, and even product quality.

UnSelling is about the big picture: creating repeat customers, not one-time buyers; creating loyal clients that refer others, not treating people like faceless numbers; becoming the go-to company for a product or service, before people even need it.

Businesses don't need social media, but they can be connecting with clients socially and they need to be listening. Brands have jumped too quickly into social without thinking and use the medium to push out messages, rather than take part in conversations. I don't believe that anyone goes online to talk to their hot dog or toilet paper. But when something goes wrong with a product like those or when someone has a great experience to share, the brand needs to be there to react. The best brands create amazing experiences and products and then make it easy for people to share them. Your video doesn't have to be viral, viewed by a million people; it just needs to be contagious in front of your specific market. Content, connection, engagement. It's time to separate from the pack of noise. That's *UnSelling*.

2

Joshie Is Branding

WE TRAVEL A lot, and we can tell you finding anything lost in a hotel is a miracle. In fact, if you yourself get lost in a hotel, you may never be found. We regularly donate phone chargers and airplane pillows to hotels. Is there some kind of underground racket for lost chargers being run out of these places? I simply refuse to be wowed by any new hotel technology as long as I am hauling furniture out of the way to find an outlet. New apps don't run on dead iPhones, you know.

When I first read the story of Joshie Hurn and his extended vacation at the Ritz-Carlton Amelia Island, a beautiful spot we've visited personally, I could not stop talking about it. A child losing his favorite thing is not something to easily manage as a parent. It's kind of like if you lost your phone.[1]

Joshie's stay at the hotel is one of my favorite stories of *UnSelling*. The care and concern of the hotel, and their treatment of a guest already checked out, is outstanding. I love to tell audiences that to be awesome in business you really only need to be mediocre, because let's be honest, everyone else sucks. Well, the Ritz-Carlton staff were way more than mediocre. They were incredible.

---

[1] I once asked a group of parents which they would rather lose at a mall: their phone or their kid. Think about it for a minute . . . the child would go back to lost and found and doesn't have your calendar and all your contacts.

Here are Chris Hurn's own words about the experience:

Most people have experienced outstanding customer service in one form or another—an attentive server at a restaurant or a retail store employee who goes the extra mile. A thriving industry comprised of consultants dedicated to training companies how to adopt exemplary customer service has blossomed over the past couple decades. For example, The Walt Disney Company Institute will help bring some of that "Disney magic" to your business.

At my company, we've always pushed our employees to go the extra mile for clients because the ripple effects of terrific customer service extend beyond mere satisfaction and retention. Exemplary customer service distinguishes your brand, builds repeat business, combats price competition, and even improves employee morale.

Hotel chain Ritz-Carlton has a storied reputation for great customer service. Many companies mimic its training programs, and one often hears executives saying they want to be known as the "Ritz-Carlton" of their respective industry, be it a law firm, car dealership or plumbing supplier.

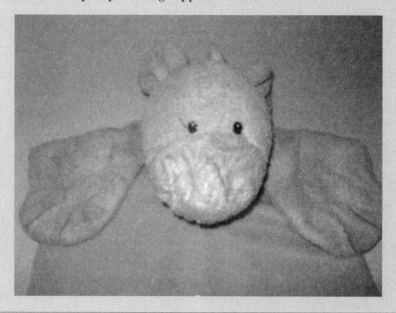

Recently, my family and I experienced the Ritz-Carlton signature customer service in a way that will be talked about in our family and at my company for many years to come. My wife and two children spent a few days at the Ritz-Carlton on Amelia Island (Florida) while I was in California on business—sadly unable to make the trip with them. Upon returning, we discovered that our son's beloved stuffed giraffe, named Joshie, had gone missing. As most parents know, children can become very attached to special blankets, teddy bears and the like. My son is extremely fond of his Joshie, and was absolutely distraught when faced with the idea of going to sleep without his favorite pal. While trying to put him to bed the first night home, I decided to tell a little white lie.

"Joshie is fine," I said. "He's just taking an extra long vacation at the resort." My son seemed to buy it, and was finally able to fall asleep, Joshie-less for the first time in a long while.

That very night, the Ritz-Carlton called to tell us they had Joshie. Thankfully, he had been found, no worse for wear, in the laundry and was handed over to the hotel's Loss Prevention Team. I came clean to the staff about the story I told my son and asked if they would mind taking a picture of Joshie on a lounge chair by the pool to substantiate my fabricated story. The Loss Prevention Team said they'd do it, and I hung up the phone very relieved.

A couple days went by, and we received a package from the hotel. It was my son's Joshie, along with some Ritz-Carlton-branded "goodies" (a frisbee, football, etc.). Also included in the package was a binder that meticulously documented his extended stay at the Ritz.

It showed Joshie wearing shades by the pool (my original request/suggestion) . . .

(continued)

(*continued*)

Joshie getting a massage at the spa . . .

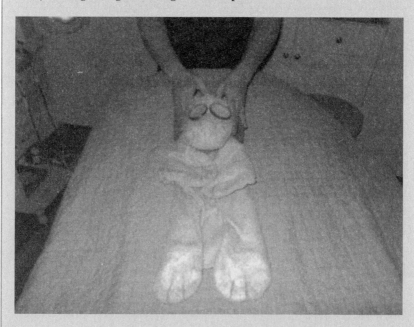

Joshie making friends with other critters . . .

(Stuffed and real) . . .[2]

---

[2]Scott here interrupting the story to let you know that that dolphin is being inappropriate. At events and conferences, please don't be the inappropriate dolphin. And, if you're standing with a group of people and don't know who the inappropriate dolphin is, then you're the inappropriate dolphin.

(continued)

(*continued*)

And Joshie driving a golf cart on the beach (who knew giraffes could drive?).

My son's Joshie was even issued a Ritz-Carlton ID badge, made an honorary member of the Loss Prevention Team, and was allowed to help by taking a shift in front of the security monitors.

THE RITZ-CARLTON®
AMELIA ISLAND

Joshie Hurn
Loss Prevention   03/25/2012

Needless to say, my wife and I were completely wowed by the Ritz-Carlton Loss Prevention Team. My son, on the other hand, didn't care so much about the binder and was just happy to have his Joshie back. I'm sure he'll have a greater appreciation for it as he grows up.

It goes without saying that the Ritz-Carlton can count on my family to be repeat customers. But I'm also telling you (and everyone else who happens to read this story). This is something I've always told my staff—create an experience so amazing that someone can't help but tell others about it, and you're sure to succeed. I'd also venture to say that Aaron (of the Ritz-Carlton Loss Prevention Team) and his cohorts had a pretty good time documenting Joshie's vacation, and employee morale is a huge part of creating a great customer experience.

All this from a stuffed giraffe who got lost on vacation.

What's one word to describe this?

Source: Reproduced by permission of Chris Hurn.

Awesome, right?

What would you do if this happened to you?[3] You would tell everyone! And he did. Did I mention that he also happens to blog for the *Huffington Post?* The Ritz-Carlton staff didn't know he did at the time. Being awesome only to influential people means you are just the opposite. The hotel treated this family as they would any other. He just happened to have a platform to share the story on—and he did.

One of the things I love about social media and the online world is that it's given us all a voice—no matter how many followers, we all have 140 characters on Twitter to share, the ability to start a blog, or friends and family to post stories to on Facebook. Stories about amazing, and horrific, customer service and products have always been shared. It's just that now, they can reach even further and matter more. Ninety percent of consumers today claim that positive online reviews influenced their buying decisions, while 86 percent said buying decisions were influenced by negative online reviews. Our voices are shaping the choices of your market.[4]

If the Ritz-Carlton had focused only on the sale, then the staff's job would have been done when the Hurn family signed out of the hotel. But they didn't. They made everything about the stay exceptional, even the loss of a cherished toy. They created an experience that mattered, that was shared, and that's what branding and marketing needs to be all about.

Joshie is what *UnSelling* is all about.

---

[3] Besides change your pants, of course.
[4] http://mklnd.com/1izaqmQ

3

Funnel Vision

MANY OF US in sales and marketing came up learning the traditional sales funnel. This was how we were supposed to think about and treat other humans—as they moved, or were converted, from hot leads and prospects to customers.

That was before social media shifted more information into the hands of our market and a negative review could spread around the world in a matter of hours.

The traditional funnel focused on sales and conversions. Once customers moved through the funnel, they were off the radar.

Today, 60 percent of all purchase decisions are made before customers enter your funnel. Consumers come to you prepared and educated, with trusted referrals in hand before they ever hear your sales pitch. Today, we can't have funnel vision. We need to look past the funnel and into what I call the sales cloud. With 74 percent of consumers relying on social networks to guide purchase decisions,[1] it's just too big to ignore.

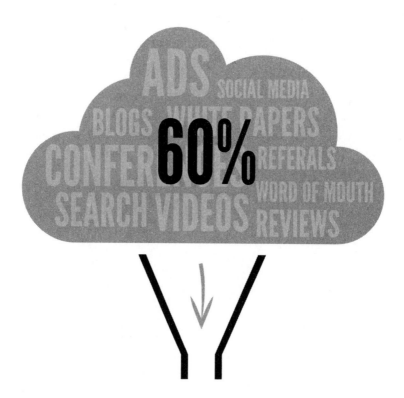

<hr />

[1]Source: http://bit.ly/SproutSocialStat

Here we see the sales cloud. It's made up of all the ways customers hear about your brand: blogs, online reviews, trusted referrals, social media sites, your website. These are where your market may or may not be hearing about you—for better or for worse. This is where most of the purchasing decisions are made. In fact, once someone is in your traditionally viewed funnel, the goal is more about not messing it up, because they've come to you with information.

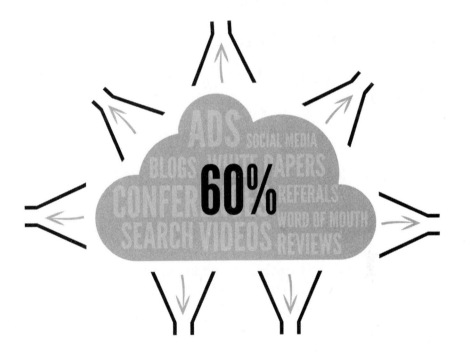

Here we see why these experiences are so important. We aren't alone as businesses; we are in competition with many other products, services, and content. In the sales cloud, people have access to a ton of information. This is why creating amazing experiences people want to share is so important—because if you aren't, someone else is. And when what's being shared about your company is negative, there is always another brand ready to make a good impression.

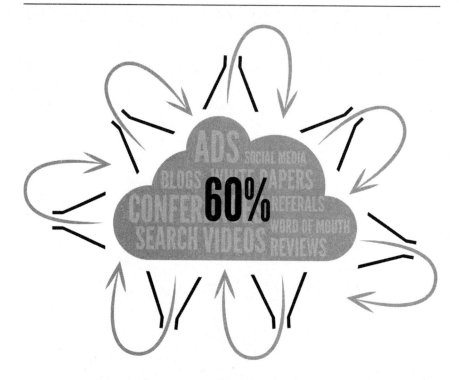

Your customers don't stop being important once they've bought from you. Once they move through your sales funnel—if you've been able to get them in and keep them happy during the process—they now reenter the sales cloud and join the other voices. Was their experience as a customer good enough to share? Did they leave unhappy? Making the sale isn't enough; we need to be creating shareable experiences for our customers through great products and service.

Once through the funnel, customers return to the cloud—this is almost always ignored. Current customers are treated as an entirely different pool than prospective ones. We bend over backward for new prospects, while leaving current customers to fend for themselves. How many times have you seen special offers made to new customers of the brands you use, only to be left without the great rate or free iPad or any other special treatment new customers have been offered? Focusing outside the funnel is what *UnSelling* is all about.

One of the arguments against valuing social media referrals is that there isn't always an easily measurable line between referral and purchase. But has there ever been? In the past, when I walked into a store to make a purchase, the salesperson never wondered whether it was my sister's recommendation, a billboard, or random chance that brought me in. Now that we can measure where a click comes from, we think that this line should be direct. Studies show that consumers will consult almost a dozen sources on average before making a purchase decision.[2] The click that leads to the sale is only a small piece of the sales puzzle.

According to data from Forrester Research, "forty-eight percent of consumers reported that social media posts are a great way to discover new products, brands, trends, or retailers, but less than 1% of transactions could be traced back to trackable social links. . . . These factoids come from consumer surveys, as well as the tracing of 77,000 online purchases made by American consumers over a two-week span in April. What researchers found is that consumers almost never buy something right after seeing it mentioned in a post by a friend or retailer on Facebook or other social media outlets."[3]

The key term here for me is that they don't buy it "right after." We have so much information before us now, that we may check 20 resources before making a click through to purchase decision. That doesn't mean that these influences aren't important or that they don't lead to decisions and purchases. It may have taken three ads, two sightings on a friend's blog, and a lot of nagging from my mom to get be to buy a new pair of jeans, but each one led to the sale with equal importance.

In today's world, we need to drop our funnel vision ways and focus on *UnSelling* if we're going to remain top of mind for our market. Buy or good-bye is ineffective in a world where purchase decisions are made long before you even get a chance pitch.

---

[2] www.thinkwithgoogle.com/collections/zero-moment-truth.html
[3] Source: http://ti.me/Q4tr2K

4

Remedies for Funnel Vision

1. Never, ever think of people as leads—online or offline. We do not walk around with invisible prospective numbers on our heads, and no one wants to be valued based on their possible future profit to you.
2. Create amazing products, services, and content first. If you put it out in the world, make it good. Social media sentiment is not to blame for your disappointing quarter; a bad product is.
3. Trusted referrals are the best marketing. When customers pass through your company funnel, they do not go live on some deserted island somewhere[1]—they go back into the mix. They share their experiences, good and bad, and those listening value these opinions ahead of any ad or campaign.

UnSelling is what happens when you understand the humanity of your market, produce a quality product, and create experiences that lead to trusted referrals. UnSelling means stepping back from the funnel and focusing on everything else but the sale. I once sat in a

---

[1]Unless you sell deserted islands, then never mind.

VIP lounge at a conference where business owners had paid extra for a few-hour closed session with me and my friend, John Morgan.[2] During the session, one person raised a hand and said, "If someone isn't ready to buy from me in the next six weeks, I don't want to talk to him. I'm not wasting my time on anyone not ready to buy." Obviously, this ray of sunshine isn't right for social media. I can't imagine anyone with that kind of attitude being great to work with at all. With so much competition and information available to our customers, who would want to work with someone who clearly just sees them as a number?

In marketing and business today, the word *experience* is used a lot. Customer experiences are shared and valued; companies work to create standout experiences for their customers to grow their businesses through social networks. As companies, we experience pushes and pulls as industries change and grow, affected by factors as varied as politics, economics, and new technologies. As consumers, our choices are continuously shaped by the experience we have with brands, some directly and some through the stories of others. The experience landscape is complicated, multifaceted, and ever changing. If you take one thing away from this book, I want it to be that experience matters in *UnSelling*. As consumers and companies, the choices we make and experiences we have and share make a difference.

There are some who disagree—who think that no matter how horrible the service, bad the product, or discriminatory the voices, there will always be customers. And there are those who think how we are treated doesn't really matter; people will just keep on buying, and any press is good press. This book is filled with case studies that show otherwise.

In *UnSelling* you will see how your experiences as a consumer matter and shape your choices and the choices of those around you, and you will see that your experiences as a business matter and can change industries and create growth. In *UnSelling*, good experience is good business.

To understand why experience matters we are going to look at what I call pulse and learn to see and break down the complicated relationship between you, your business and your industry, and the market around you.

---

[2]http://johnmichaelmorgan.com/

5

Pulse

THE RELATIONSHIP BETWEEN a brand and its market is complex and always changing. To succeed in the sales cloud, we need to figure out how our interactions with customers and potential customers are shaped. Understanding this relationship is the first step in *UnSelling* called the *pulse*.

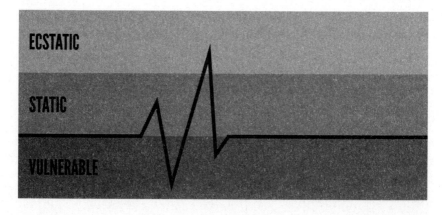

In the fancy picture shown here the line represents a person experiencing a brand. This is called the *pulse line*. It moves up or down depending on how the individual is feeling about the brand.

The brand space is the background, made up of three possibilities: *vulnerable, static,* and *ecstatic.* The lowest, vulnerable, is where people are most open to competition. They may not have made a purchase decision yet, or they may just be unhappy with past interactions. As companies we work hard to move people out of this space.

In the middle we have *current static customers.* This is the space where companies have the greatest direct effect on customer experience—for good and bad. Here we see interactions such as "great customer service experience" or "frustrating return policy" as the customer and brand interact. There is never a neutral brand experience; we are always either moving up or down in relation to how we feel about the brand.

At the top we have *ecstatic customers.* Here we have our brand fans and ambassadors. Competitors can't touch us up here. Static customers exist, but ecstatic customers refer. We should be doing everything we can, every single day in business to move individuals into this space.

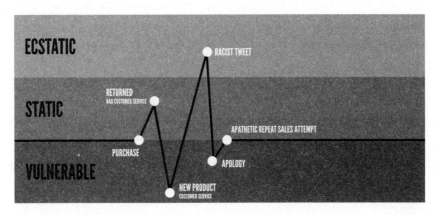

Each point of contact between brand and individual is called a *pulse point.*[1] This is where we can measure the relationship between the brand and its market at any time. Because there is no such thing as a neutral brand experience, the line is always moving. In this image, we see pulse points such as *purchase* and *new product,* both of which raise

---

[1]Most graphs are the opposite of this. Each data point usually comes after the rise/fall, to show how far up/down sentiment has gone. We've done the opposite on purpose. To show that everything was going one direction, until the pivot took place.

the pulse in this case. We also see points such as *bad customer service* and *racist tweet*, both of which brought the pulse down.

When the bottom falls out on pulse, we see a *flatline*. This is the definitive end of the relationship and an opportunity for competitors. The flatline is very important in social media because it is extreme. Extreme experiences, both good and bad, are always shared the most online. When a flatline happens, people will take to social media and other sales cloud kinds of communication, such as blogs and review sites, to share their horror stories.

To understand how the pulse moves, we need to look at two factors: external and internal. *External factors* are outside the control of the pulse line, meaning that these are forces from the brand, not within the control of the individual. The pulse points described earlier are all external factors.

The *internal factors* are those inside the control of the individual, such as purchase decisions and reactions to the brand. Internal factors can be understood by breaking them down into three types, what I call *AIM*. AIM is where the customer is headed and is made up of aspiration, information, and motivation.

In the next chapters of this book, we are going to look at all these parts of pulse in more detail, using some of my favorite examples of businesses doing things right and a few whose customer pulse could never be saved.

6

Air Canada versus WestJet

I TRAVEL AROUND the world speaking to audiences about social media, which means I live in airports and hotels. Oversized carry-on suitcases make all my pet peeve lists, and I know which airlines and which planes have the best seats and where. Most of my flights come out of Canada, from Toronto Pearson Airport, where two Canadian airlines battle it out for loyalty: WestJet and Air Canada.

I started out an Air Canada fan. It had a great loyalty program, which meant all my flying time brought me the option of a comfy lounge for long stopovers and lots of seat upgrade points. With a lot of travel, comes a lot of changes — time zones, food, beds, and so on — and keeping airlines steady meant at least the getting there and getting home part could remain predictable. And anything predictable on the road is worth a ton. Within a year, I'd reached Super Elite status and was a loyal customer. Well done, Air Canada. Well done.

And then things began to slip. With each interaction, my pulse as a customer plummeted, leaving me open to competition. I moved from the ecstatic customer category to being wide open to Air Canada competitors. Over the past two years, as the airline was steadily losing my loyalty, I've actually started keeping a running tally of flights we've

21

booked on WestJet. And trust me, two years of flights, mostly business class, are adding up. So far we're at $15,000 in five months.

First, there was Air Canada's manager of corporate communications, Peter Fitzpatrick, who holds the precious spot above Moron Mountain. If you aren't familiar with the infamous UnPodcast[1] staple, check out Chapter 54, but basically he is our least favorite businessperson. Ever. For several offenses. These include but are not limited to sending out an e-mail meant to be internal, where he brushed aside concerns of a customer whose dog had been lost during travel and was killed. The dog had been safely crated for the trip, with instructions not to let it out for walks. And then, he was let out for a walk. Nothing like a horrible e-mail gone public to show your true colors. He was also the head of the public relations nightmare we faced a few years ago when a good friend's nephew's wheelchair was broken by the airline. Then we heard about its policy on transferring ticket vouchers, which will not allow one to be transferred between family members if they do not share the last name. I am not sure which century Air Canada thinks they are operating in, but that policy is archaic.[2]

The launch of Rouge really pushed me over the customer edge pulse-wise. Rouge is meant as a more modern, lower cost airline. Flights are given Air Canada flight numbers but shown as operated by Rouge. I have been totally unimpressed with the service. Some TripAdvisor reviews include all-caps *AWFULS* and stories of how customers end up booked on Rouge flights without realizing it. First-class tickets are sold for seats no wider or more comfortable than regular ones—but at the higher first-class price, of course. Stories of seat changes, which we experienced personally, made without notification, are all over travel review websites and social media.

Meanwhile, on the other side of the epic battle for our seats in the sky, we have WestJet, Air Canada's main competitor in Canada. When a flight booked through WestJet was cancelled, we received text and e-mail notification early enough to save ourselves a trip to the airport. When planes have been changed before flights in the past, we've received notices about things like changes in onboard entertainment systems. Now we may travel with two iPads, phones, and laptops,

---

[1]Check out UnPodcast.com
[2]Source: http://bit.ly/ACLastName

but for some, a trip without in-flight entertainment can be a nightmare. Why not let customers know before the flight and save them, and your flight attendants, the hassle of needing to manage that kind of stressful, preventable situation?

Although Air Canada has no problem using our e-mail addresses to share promotions, they do not send out notifications about seat and flight changes. When asked why, the response is simple: It's not something they do. So that's it then?

Brand tolerance can only go so far. I stayed with Air Canada because of their loyalty program and because, to me, direct flights trump all things in travel. But with a brand voice like Peter Fitzpatrick's, stories of lost pets during travel, horrible treatment both personally and to friends, and a lack of contact about changes to travel, we start to see brand erosion. Add in the mix another option—a competitor ready to take our business on in stride—and you have a huge change in pulse.

External pulse factors like the ones I experience as a airline customer can feel very much out of our control. We feel bounced around by what's going on around us, as though brands are entirely in control of our experience with them. When control should really be with us, we're often at the mercy of bad customer service and product issues.

There isn't a day that goes by when someone isn't sharing a story about being treated poorly as a customer. These are the external factors affecting the pulse line, and they are all about the company and how it decides to operate. It's become so bad that we expect to be treated badly by businesses and even mediocre experiences have become exceptional.

Some examples of external factors include:

- Product quality
- Customer service
- Response time to questions and concerns
- Cost
- Convenience
- Social media personality
- Brand stances on various issues of importance to the customer

As consumers, we make choices about how we feel about a brand based on these factors. For every person, just how important these factors are varies. You may have sworn off a certain store because of a bad experience or store policy, but if it builds a new location next door to your work, then convenience may become important enough to ignore the rest.

Other more broad external factors include government regulations, such as ESRB rating video games for age appropriateness, which affect choices available to the market.[3] International regulations, such as those controlling trade, can limit what companies can and cannot offer customers. Industry trends, such as unpaid internships, can put pressure on our own company practices. Economic and governmental changes affect us as well. With every company we interviewed in preparing for this book, the economic downturn played a large part in their decision making.

As I was going over this chapter on a recent WestJet flight before submitting the manuscript to my publisher, a WestJet executive, Ed Baklor, VP of Guest Services boarded the plane. I knew he was from the airline, because I was sitting in the front row and he introduced himself to the flight attendant, Suzanne. He let her know he'd be helping with service on the flight.

I didn't think much about it at the time, until I saw him get up once the seatbelt sign turned off and start helping serve drinks to everybody. It was as if he thought his job as an executive should include making sure the customer was happy with their choice of brand or something.

I later asked Suzanne about the experience and whether it was surprising to her. I certainly had never seen any other executive on any other flight with any other airline ever help with service. She answered no, that all of WestJet's executives are like this. It had started with their founder, Clive Beddoe, and trickled down through the company from there.

Passion is contagious. Check WestJet's Twitter account: @WestJet. This company is the definition of engagement and social listening. Staff cheer with brand fans and act quickly when customers hit a speed bump on their brand runway. Every step of the way, they've continued to make me more and more confident in my choice of airlines.

Air travel is one of the most stressful times for many, and airlines have an opportunity to separate themselves from the competition by

[3] Source: http://bit.ly/UnSRB

making it as smooth and painless as possible. With each interaction, or pulse point, along the way, Air Canada had an opportunity. The company had done all the work, and I was already at the ecstatic customer level. Every interaction, from the online stories of its communications manager extraordinaire, to every time I sat down in one of its seats, had the chance to keep the pulse moving up. Unfortunately for Air Canada, each point only moved me closer and close to a WestJet seat, where I continue to fly, 25 flights and counting.

7

External Pulse Factors and Trends

SHERYL SANDBERG'S BEST-SELLING book *Lean In* was hard to avoid in 2013. Whether you loved it or hated it, no one seemed to be able to miss the message to women in the business world: Work hard, press for recognition and success, and don't be afraid to demand more compensation for your good work.

The Facebook bigwig was already worth an estimated $400 million, and the book only added to that success. Let's just say, whether you agree or not, the lean in philosophy sure seems to be working for her.

So in August, when Jessica Bennett, *Lean In*'s editor/producer, posted to Facebook that she was looking for an intern, you can image it was shared like crazy online. And it was. But not for the reason you might first think.

> Wanted: Lean In editorial intern, to work with our editor (me) in New York. Part-time, unpaid, must be HIGHLY organized with editorial and social chops and able to commit to a regular schedule through end of year. Design and web skills a plus! HIT ME UP. Start date ASAP.

Seeking out and expecting people to work unpaid—and to be worked hard—doesn't exactly scream the Lean In message! The post went viral. The group attempted to reshape the request, claiming to be a nonprofit group seeking a volunteer, but with word being out regarding just how much money the book and author had made, the idea of comparing herself to a nonprofit did not go over well.

Too many young workers are quick to take unpaid internships to gain experience. The issue is that most of these kinds of internships are illegal, and workplaces are taking advantage of workers who would be much better utilized in paid positions. It also sets a tone where companies are competing for good employees against things like this.

As explained in Business Insider, "The only people—women, in this case—who can afford to take unpaid internships are rich women, or women with rich parents, who don't need to be paid. Poor women won't be able to respond to the Lean In ad, no matter how much they want to support Sandberg's program. And they are the very people who would most benefit from having Lean In on their resumes and perhaps a personal reference from Sandberg herself."[1]

Our favorite post about this topic came from Jeni Marinucci, author of the *Highly Irritable Blog*. You can read the original post at http://bit.ly/UnBarrelSuit.

Unpaid Internships Are the New Barrel Suit

I am looking for work. When I am looking for work, looking for work *is* my work. I send the kids to school, fire up the computer, and then I go online in search of employment suitable for my experience and educational background. I don't have high expectations. I would like a short commute or a work-from-home position; I expect a reasonable amount of courtesy in communication; and I would like to be challenged and given room to expand my skill-set. Oh, and I would like **to be paid**.

It is this last point—the "paid" part—where I generally run into trouble. I am a recent University graduate from a

(continued)

---

[1] Source: http://bit.ly/UnIntern

(*continued*)

well-respected school and I have a decent portfolio and references who will tell you you're a fool not to hire me. I am professional, I work hard, and frankly, I am a fucking joy to be around. I usually find several jobs per day for which I could apply. So why don't I? *Because they are unpaid.* Zip. *Zilch.* **Zero.** Yep; they are "Thanks for everything; here's your nothing" jobs. Great! I'll use my nonexistent pay cheque to buy invisible kids shoes and some ghost groceries.

I can't count all the ways these types of job postings state they are "sadly, unpaid at this time." It's actually funny in a lot of cases, because the responsibilities and qualifications are laid out and described *exactly like a paying job*—sometimes even resembling pretty intense, high-level responsibility jobs. The slam comes below the fold, after you're hooked, because this one? This one sounds like the one, you guys! I'm not against internships of all stripes. I think internships can be a great way to learn about an industry, and time spent interning can be a great addition to a resume which also includes paid experience and educational training. Networking and showcasing your talent is a good thing, but hey, why not pay people *something* for it? Even a pittance. *Something.*

If unpaid internships are offered as part of an educational program—say, a University degree, or college diploma program—then they are useful and often act as a springboard for a career in that field. Auto mechanics, welders, and other trades people often work in their chosen field between bouts of schooling, and they are almost always paid for their labour. Their wages may not be commensurate with their responsibilities at that particular point in the career evolution cycle, but they can look forward to fair wages (hopefully) once they receive a trade ticket. If a company is willing to pay an intern "at some point in the future" for the same work they are doing now "provided they meet our (subjective?) standard" then PAY THEM NOW, JERK.

Summer internships and those specifically for students are sometimes unpaid. Okay; if they're not full time then a student can generally work as well, or perhaps the student is also able to live on student loans, etc. Because I am a writer, I have been searching the editorial/creative field for work and I am shocked—SHOCKED I TELL YOU—at the amount of work I've seen which is compensated solely in "experience" and "exposure." This no-pay structure comes through the abundance of internships or because those seeking the material or content do not wish to pay *anything* to a creator.

I was married to a business owner. I know how difficult and costly it can be to get a business up and running. I know that business owners often do not take a salary themselves until a profit has been turned. But I also know that not one single utility company, fuel provider, tax accountant, restaurant, cleaning person, maintenance company, delivery service, dog walker or liquor store will provide you with services and/or products free of charge for promise of "giving them a platform upon which their work will be exposed to hundreds of people." If that were the case, I'd be chugging Chilean Merlot in a strip mall parking lot and yelling into car windows how this stuff is *the best goddamn wine I've ever tasted so Shop at Bob's Liq-R-Mart!*

I am "old" (by comparison) in a vast sea of debt-riddled new graduates. But the young ones can't afford to work for free either. In fact, it may be worse for them because life hasn't yet sanded smooth the edges of their hopefulness and they are still sickeningly full of optimism. I have some equity and it is likely I won't starve to death if I cannot find full-time work soon. Job-searching is soul-crushing at the best of times and I honestly don't know how young graduates—kids!—pay their rent. I understand why so many have to move back in with parents and I really hope the climate changes by the time my kids graduate, although my daughter is headed for a science/math degree and no one wants an unpaid engineer building their bridges so she'll likely find work. I don't want to regret my English/History degree because it shaped my thinking and I call upon the analytical skills it enforced every single day. But when I am being brutally honest

(continued)

(*continued*)

with myself I admit I'm tempted to visit every University Fair within a 50 mile radius and tell all prospective Liberal Arts students to "RUN FOR YOUR FUCKING LIVES!"

I am a decent writer. I have even been told that I am sometimes a pretty good one, and I believe it. That's not hubris. There are a lot of things I don't do well and that list is much longer than the one of things I *can* do. I would never apply to nursing school. I would never try to get a job as a school bus driver, or a server in a bar, because I wouldn't do those things well and my exit would likely be marked by lots of flames and probably a lawsuit. I write, I edit, I social media-lize. I don't posture myself as a Nora Ephron, or an Anne Lamott. I am Jeni Marinucci, and I would like to be paid.

The trend of unpaid internships and exchange for reviews, writing, design and other services devalues quality and the efforts of those who create it. As I've said many times over the years, the best marketing you can do for your business is to hire well. If you want your business to stand out for products and service people love, you need to invest in your employees. You can't expect the best employees for a promise of exposure or experience. Hire for passion and treat employees with value and respect—that way when you get what you pay for, you'll be getting awesome work, instead of a whole lot of nothing.

Source: Reproduced by permission of Jeni Marinucci.

This trend of exchanging work for exposure or experience is a dangerous kind of external pulse factor. It devalues work. It takes advantage of those just getting started or who are in disadvantaged situations. And from a business perspective, it does not lead to the best people being placed in the best positions. Free labor is bad for business, period. Your employees are your best marketers, and they should not be treated as a commodity to be wrung dry for as little cost as possible.

8

Our Return Policy Is for You Not to Return

I GET WHY stores have policies. I understand why return policies require customers to have receipts to return merchandise in exchange for cash. I've worked in retail on the floor and on the corporate side. But what happened to me a few years ago at a Zellers is the perfect example of how policy that might prevent a small amount of shrinkage[1] can lose you a lot of customers.

I had purchased a giant jug of water for our dispenser at home at a local Zellers. I didn't usually shop at this location but happened to be in the area and had to grab a few things. Since these jugs are the size of the earth on the shoulders of Atlas, they demand a $10 deposit so you'll barrel-roll it back in when it's empty and presumably grab a new one at the same store, creating a magical water circle of life where you buy from them forever!

Because the customer service staff were the only ones in the store authorized to dispense this level of cash to me, I got in line with my

---

[1] "I WAS IN THE POOL!"—George Costanza

jug at the customer service desk. I waited for about 10 minutes and then approached the desk, eagerly anticipating my newfound wealth. I caber-tossed the jug on top of the counter and mentioned I was returning it for my deposit. The employee asked for a copy of my receipt, which I didn't have on me. Since it had taken us a few months to get through the 9,384 gallons of jug water, I hadn't even thought of keeping it. I wasn't returning it because it was faulty or tasted like Sprite;[2] I was simply returning it for my deposit back.

She looked at me like I was a hooligan. She then uttered, "We need the receipt to prove you bought it from us." I just stared for a second, trying to comprehend how else I would have obtained an empty Zellers water jug. Was there an underground cartel of water jug counterfeit manufacturers? Was there a small, but blessed with massive hands, gang that carried out home invasions and their desired loot were gargantuan water bottles?

Again I told her that I didn't have the receipt, and she rolled her eyes and let me know that she would have to give me a store credit instead. Not a huge problem, because I had to pick up a few things anyway, but now I was angry on principle. I agreed to it, though. I was here, after all, jug in hand, and I just wanted to get rid of the thing and get out of there.

That's when she asked me for some ID.

I wish I could describe the look on my face by this point. It was a combination of anger, confusion, sadness, and joy that I would one day be able to tell this story in book form. I asked her to repeat herself, and she confirmed that she would need a government-issued identification to process the return of the empty water jug in order to give me a $10 store credit. Obviously I had to ask her why. She replied, "We need to make sure people aren't returning these and abusing the system."

By this point, all my will to argue and point out common sense had drained from me. Dehydration and idiocy had won and gave her my driver's license. I assume I am now in the delinquent deposit-seeking database, and if I return one more, I may appear on the Zellers most-returned list, faxed to all the stores as a warning.

---

[2]Obviously, I would have kept and refilled this mystical Sprite-creating jug had I had one of those.

From what I can gather, the policy was created for overall returns of merchandise without receipt. I know this is a huge issue for stores, and a good policy to have to prevent bad returns and employee theft. However, this umbrella policy only served to anger customers and treat loyal ones like thieves if they left their paperwork at home.

I was so frustrated by the time I'd traded my jug for $10 in store credit that I didn't even spend the gift card. I walked out of the store empty-handed. Looking back, this kind of makes me the loser here. Guess I showed them?

As I walked out of Zellers that day, a bit dazed from the experiences and exhausted from jug slinging, I knew I wouldn't be going back there. Although I probably should have used the store credit, I had more on my list for the day than $10 in stuff. The jug had brought me back into the store, but the policy experience had been so bad that it prevented me from making any further purchases. The return policy was a preventive policy—so bad that it took my experience with the company for a nosedive, all the way to a pulse flatline.

When one Samsung customer's phone caught fire, he tried to find resolution with the company and was asked for proof. Samsung can't just replace every single burned-up Galaxy S4! Think of how many people try to take advantage of them!

And so the customer made a video to prove his honesty. What better way to prove to them that his phone fire had been legit? What the company wasn't counting on, of course, was that the video would also be shared on YouTube. There the proof was clear, complete with a melted charging port, for Samsung and the world to see.

Samsung replied to the video and offered the customer, Ghostlyrich on YouTube, a new phone if he agreed to take down the video and assure the company that he wouldn't upload another like it. They also told him he would need to sign (with a witness) away any right he had to sue them and never share the details of how he got his new S4 with the world.

The YouTuber had different ideas. He shared the entire experience with his audience, along with the company's wishes to hide the serious safety issues with its product. As I write this today, the second video had 1.4 million views.

Talk about a policy—and then attempt at censorship—gone wrong!

I can image the meeting at Samsung to discuss how to handle the pesky YouTuber. Rather than simply get in touch with him to apologize and make things right, they decided to try to censor him. If a phone company has an issue with phones catching on fire, maybe pushing customers to be quiet about it isn't the best use of their time.[3]

Policies are necessary in certain scenarios. That's why we create them. But blanket policies put into place without context only end up hurting employees and customers alike. And please, never, ever answer a customer question of why with the two worst words in business: "It's policy." That's a surefire way to send any customer pulse into the ground.

[3]Source: http://bit.ly/SamsungFire

9

Taking the Customer Pulse

In UnMarketing, we talked about a system to check in on customer sentiment called Stop, Start, Continue. We asked our current customers three questions: What would you like us to stop doing? What would you like us to start doing? What would you like us to continue doing? The answers to these three simple questions give us a good picture of where we're sitting with our market and how we can improve. We need to be asking these questions and listening to the answers. This is the real brand statement for our business, more than any fancy framed motto we hang on our office wall.

We need to be taking the pulse of our customers, paying attention to how our actions are affecting their choices and the way our brand is being represented in the sales cloud. We can do this by looking at external pulse factors—the push and pull on the pulse line—taking customers from vulnerable to static and ecstatic and back down again.

External factors affect the pulse from the outside in. They pull the line up or push it down, taking the customer on what can be a bumpy brand ride. These are controlled by the brand; product quality, customer service, and public relations are all external factors affecting customer experience.

When customers come to us with an issue they're having with our product or service, there are two possible reactions we can have: It's our problem, or it's not our problem. All too often, issues are met with each and every attempt at dismissal. You've called the wrong number, you're in the wrong line, you need to do x before we can help you. As customers, we hear these excuses every day. It seems like whomever we are speaking to will do just about anything to *not* help us.

One of the simplest ways to improve the customer service of your business, and therefore the happiness of your customers, is to let their concerns be your problem. That doesn't mean every employee needs to have a resolution for every issue. It means that every point of contact should be part of leading to the solution. Sometimes this can be as easy as connecting customers to the right department, rather than just sending them off with a new number and little hope.

Other external factors are competition. How are our competitors treating the market? What options are they providing that might affect their experience with us? Customers may be satisfied with a certain product or service, until they see there is a better one available or another pain point is being solved somewhere else.

T-Mobile struck a chord with their competition's customers when they launched a new program—the Uncarrier 4.0 initiative[1] —offering to pay off any early termination fees for users who switched to their service. Mobile customers who are unhappy with their contracts will often feel forced to stay in them because of the high fees for ending a contract early. T-Mobile knew this and decided to make a bold step toward stealing these unhappy customers away. They saw the early termination fee as an external factor ruining customer experience and decided to provide a happy, less costly alternative.

T-Mobile asks prospective customers to "write their break-up letter" to their current mobile provider and share it with others: "If you're feeling stuck in a contract with no way out, or scared to leave thanks to big ETFs, we feel you. It's OK to want out. Remember, it's them—not you." You can even see which companies others have broken up with on the "who's dumping who" page. The approach is perfect for the market T-Mobile is after. This isn't the first time it has focused on common pain points in its industry to steal customers from

---

[1] http://bit.ly/UnCarrier

the competition. T-Mobile also lets users upgrade their phones earlier than other plans and offers free international roaming.

Internal Customer Factors and AIM

In the end, as businesses we do not determine customer choices—they do. Purchasing decisions are made based on a variety of factors, not all of which we are always able to affect. What will lead one person to swear off a brand may barely affect another and in some cases even lead to brand loyalty.

"I just felt like a change and wanted to try something new."

"We moved to a new house and needed a grocery store nearby."

"We took up a new sport and need all the gear."

"My son has an allergy, and we need products to help."

These are all examples of internal, individual factors that shape the pulse. Each will affect the experience a person has with a brand. Once the brand no longer meets these internal needs, no matter what it does, the pulse will suffer. On the other hand, a person can quickly become an ecstatic customer when these internal factors are met.

Individual characteristics such as age and location all shape our decisions. We don't want to place our marketing efforts ahead of the customer curve. A millennial customer with an iPhone is going to have different patterns than a senior who reads the newspaper every night. They may both be potential customers, but how we reach them may differ.

Proximity or convenience is a huge internal factor. We will put up with a lot of things—bad service, mediocre quality—and even ignore competitors all because a brand is close by or easy to access. That's why thinking about how our customers want to consume our content or purchase our products and/or services is so important. When was the last time you tried to buy something from your own company? How was the experience? Making customers jump through unnecessary hoops is dangerous in a world where online sales are made in minutes and delivered in hours. Test out how your customers experience your store and website, even your newsletter. It shouldn't be a workout to buy from you.

Marketers are customers. We are all customers. And in *UnSelling* we recognize that purchasing decisions are being affected by social voices more and more. As we've been talking about, there are external and internal factors affecting our customers' experience all the time, moving the pulse from vulnerable to ecstatic.

10

Are You in the Customer Tolerating Business?

WE SEE DATA all the time: Sales are up, sales are down, here are the external factors why. Companies will point to factors seemingly outside of their control, as though we aren't all a part of creating the environment we work in. They may even sometimes mention internal factors, but they never mention individual factors.

Individual actions = External results

There is no better way can I explain this than by telling you about the time I tried to buy some overpriced headphones in Best Buy.

My two oldest kids were in the market for Beats by Dre headphones. Being 16 and 12 at the time, how they look is paramount to how they sound, and apparently cost is irrelevant. With saved-up gift cards and birthdays within calendar range, we headed out to pick up two pairs of these life-changing devices.

Since Best Buy was close by and the gift cards were from there, we decided to pop in, ready to purchase. We were looking for only the most basic form of customer service: the one where the purchase decision

39

had already been made and we just needed someone, anyone, to take our money.

We walked through the store and located the headphones on our own, finding them enclosed in the kind of glass case usually reserved for atomic-grade plutonium and royal jewels. Excitedly, we stood there for a few minutes looking like we wanted to buy them, since we couldn't open the case without help. During the wait, no less than five employees passed us without making eye contact—most likely on purpose.

We tried to stop the sixth, who was quite taken aback because, as he let us know, the headphones were not in his section. He then pointed at the employee who we were meant to see, who was currently helping another customer. Number Six left us to wait and assumed that Section Guy would be with us soon. All we needed was someone with a key. We had done our research, had committed to a product decision, and could see the freaking product in front of us, just out of reach—and yet, no dice.

After Number Six walked away, still no one was available to help us for the next 5 minutes. It may not seem like long to you, but waiting in an aisle with two kids while looking like a moron, felt like forever. So, much to the embarrassment of the kids, I decided it was time to get some attention and started yodeling—literally.

My yodeling took the kids from laughing to horrified in less than 60 seconds, and still no one came. The best part of the whole thing: I tweeted from the aisle of the store that I was yodeling in Best Buy and someone from Best Buy's Twitter account replied to me before anyone in the store came to help us. The account rep wanted to know how he could help, and all I could say back was, "I just want to give you my money."

After a grand total of 15 minutes, I put down the DVDs I didn't need, gave one last look to the glass-enclosed headphones, and left. We had left my eldest's phone at the Apple Store for a fix, so we headed there and grabbed the headphones at the same time. Within moments, a salesperson was by our side, ready to check us out.

This was a $600 purchase that will never come up on Best Buy's analytics, shareholder reports, or business analysis. Even though there were similar headphones out on their shelves, they'd chosen to lock these away, without making sure there would always be an employee on hand to open the case—you know . . . to sell the headphones!

Retail stores complain about showrooming, a term defined as looking at products in store and then ordering them online, and yet when we are in their stores, they do nothing to make us want to shop there.

When sales are down, companies will look for blame in a number of ways. Here is how we can understand these in terms of *UnSelling*, looking at our experience at Best Buy:

- *External factor blame:* People showroom rather than buy in store. The Internet has killed store sales. Nothing we can do.
- *Internal factor blame:* It's policy to lock up expensive or desired products; otherwise, people will steal them. We need to prevent crime. That's the most important thing.
- *Individual factor:* It's not my problem. It's not my department. If it wasn't for these pesky customers, it would be so much easier to get this job done.

Blaming everything but a rude, undersupported, and understaffed sales team is an easy way out for companies. When, in fact, it is great individual factors, such as great frontline workers, that can make all the difference, even in the face of external and internal factors like those just described. It has gotten to the point where the only objection to buying online is shipping time—and just how long do you think it will be before we mark shipping times in hours rather than in days?

Frontline workers are your most valuable and usually your most undervalued employees. And that is a huge problem, especially when we're looking at pulse and how points of contact with brands are always moving our experience with them up or down. When we value each contact not only as a sale but also as an opportunity to reach others with great stories about our brand, we can't allow the Best Buy yodeling situation to happen. Not because of online shopping or theft prevention—not for anything.

If you don't provide knowledgeable and effective service in retail, you lose your entire competitive advantage.

Knowledge + Passion for product/service = Profit

Next time you see someone yodeling in your store, maybe give the person a hand.

11

Internal Factors and AIM

WHERE WE'RE AIMING is important. It's important because it shapes our experience and pulse and also because it's something we can control. As consumers, we have goals in mind for what we expect when we purchase a product or service from a company. The goals can include quality, good value, and a certain quality of rightness with who we see ourselves as. For example, if we are buying a car, we aim to meet goals such as fuel efficiency, a car loan we can afford, and something that makes us look cool when we take our kids to school. Therefore, automotive companies market their cars based on convincing us their car will meet these expectations better than any other company's. Marketing is really about presenting the expectations people have in mind.

For *UnSelling,* we are going to break AIM up into three components:

1. Aspiration
2. Information
3. Motivation

Aspiration

Who do we want to be? Advertisers and marketers spend a lot of time focusing on creating that image—the one where our ideal selves are using their clients' products: a sports car driver, a gym member, a Google employee, a Yale student. As individuals we tend to have an image in mind of who we want to present to the world, and understanding that is key. Brands with strong stories and identities make it easy for us to fit them into our own aspirations. As a company, you also have aspirations that shape how you make decisions. Do you want to be the go-to brand in your industry? Or do you want to be the local company known to support community development?

Information

Data is everywhere, and what data we have shapes our decisions. That makes data a powerful and sometimes problematic tool. Information is so easily bent and filtered toward certain conclusions that we need to be skeptical and inform ourselves before using any one piece of data when making decisions. This is true as consumers, and also as companies as we will see later when we look more in depth into the dangers of bad data for your business.

Motivation

Why are we doing the things we do? Are we looking to make charitable choices or help the environment? Motivation sets up our aspirations and answers the why to who we see ourselves being. We aspire to be an iPhone owner, because we are motivated by wanting to have a phone with access to a certain collection of apps and quality customer service from a man with a beard and plaid shirt. The best kind of product creation (and content creation for that matter) is about finding a why that hasn't been answered and answering it. If we can answer a question and fill a need for our market, we'll always be needed.

12

Aspiring to Be a Jedi

ASPIRATION IS OUR hope to obtain something to take our story and bring it to a place we want to be. It shapes the way our pulse moves and how we make decisions. When we make purchases, we are asking ourselves if we want to be associated with these decisions. Are you a Windows or a Mac, for example? On the other side, branding and marketing is about a company making a promise to your customers to meet their expectations.

If a brand fits with our aspirations, we are much more likely to put up with certain disappointments. For example, I just told you the story about Beats by Dr. Dre headphones and how they had me yodeling in Best Buy. Well, a few months after UnJr got his headphones home, they broke. The plastic on one side snapped. Since I'd paid quite a bit, and gone through a book chapter's worth of effort to attain these headphones, I decided to get in touch with the company and find out what we could do. The company was awesome, and the person I spoke to let me know how I could send back in the broken headphones for a new pair, and all before Dr. Dre could make another comeback.

When I was figuring the whole process out, I did a bit of research into the product and it turns out that the headphones break this way often—maybe a little too often considering the price of the things.

So the great customer service by them was no doubt needed to keep a lot of parents and trendy kids happy. And that brings us to the big question: Would we buy another pair of Beats headphones knowing the product issues? The answer is yes. We would because these are the headphones UnJr wants, because of aspiration. The company has done a brilliant job of being one of the brands kids think of when they think "cool headphones."

What about as a company. Do we see ourselves as a creative, modern design firm or as a local, family-friendly restaurant? Do we aspire to be known as environmentally friendly or cutting edge? When I speak about branding, I talk a lot about how your mission statement isn't what you say it is—but what your customer says. The first thing that comes to mind for your market when they hear your brand is your mission statement. Save yourself the framing cost for the fancy statement on your office wall and ask your customers.

What we can do is ask ourselves what we hope our customers will reply and then work toward creating experiences that facilitate that response. So if we want to be known as a company that puts the customer first, we need to make that happen by actually putting that in place. We need to hire better and staff our customer service lines. We need to empower employees to make good decisions. Actions become our brand statement.

Disney is a brand that comes to mind. A few months ago, we went on Facebook and Twitter and posted:

> We are knee deep in research for book #4 UnSelling and have a question for you. When you hear Disney, what is the first thing you think of?

The post was seen by over 15,000 people. And we received a ton of responses, 347 on Facebook to be exact. The responses varied from "the mouse" to "amazing customer service" to a handful of angry calls of racism, sexism, and horrible princesses. The vast majority of the replies were positive, and most of the negative statements were about cost.

When someone says "Disney," what is the first thing that comes to mind for you? For us, the answer is magic. And here is one of our favorite stories to explain why. You can read the original post on Sharon's blog: http://bit.ly/UnDisney.

Dear Master Jedi,

This is an open letter of deep appreciation to you. I hope that somehow it finds its way to your computer screen.

You are an actor, and a damn funny one to boot. You're really skilled at working with the unpredictability of kids and turning it into entertainment. I really hope that when you auditioned for and won this gig, that you've been as pleased with your job as your audiences have been with your performance. I also hope that this leads to bigger and better things, if that's what you choose. You're a supremely decent man and I'm ever in your debt for how you helped me out Tuesday, June 4th at the end of the last show of the day.

You see, during the months of planning for our Disneyworld trip, I found out about the Jedi Training Academy in Hollywood Studios and knew that my little boy would LOVE participating in it. He has been diagnosed with autism, and is typically oblivious to what goes on around him—except for Star Wars. I found an online clip of the Jedi Academy that some parent uploaded and showed him. He was so excited!

"I want to do that! I want to fight Darth Vader!"

He so very seldom really communicates with us that when he does, I move heaven and earth to keep that connection going. He wanted to fight Darth Vader, huh? Then by God, he would.

When we arrived at Hollywood Studios at the ribbon drop, I high-tailed it to sign up for the Jedi Training. There was already a huge line, and I was a little worried that all the spots would fill up before we reached the front of it. I was also concerned because the workers at the front were asking the KIDS questions to ascertain if they can follow instructions. I squatted down and had a little pep talk with my boy.

"Josiah, look at me, please. Look at me. Good. Listen to me. Are your ears on? Good. That lady is going to ask you how old you are. Do you know how old you are? Eight! That's right! Now, you HAVE to talk to her, OK? I mean it, sweetie. When she talks to you, you talk back, or she won't let you fight Darth Vader."

He never gave any sign of recognition, but I hoped that he understood. We've been working on appropriate conversation skills for months now, and I was counting on that therapy to kick in high gear for him in this moment.

It's our turn! Here we go.

"Hello and good morning!" said a bright and cheery Disney cast member to Josiah. (They are ALL bright and cheery.) "Are you ready to battle the Dark Side?"

"Yes." Josiah mumbled.

Oh my God! He talked to her!

"Good! We need brave Jedis like you. How old are you?"

Josiah hesitated. She asked him again. I was about to answer for him when he said, "I eight."

Yes!

"Eight. That's great! Now, can you follow directions?"

Josiah blinked at her.

"If I told you to raise your hands, what would you . . . Good!"

Josiah had risen his hands up high before she finished her question.

Because of this miracle of a "conversation" we were able to secure two spots for both of our kids in the 8:00 show. (our daughter decided she wanted to be a Jedi too) Perfect! This is going to be something they'll remember their entire life!

After signing up, we went about our sight-seeing of the park—riding Star Tours 3 times in the process. Before and after each ride or attraction, my son asked, "Am I going to fight Darth Vader now?"

"No." I'd reply. "After supper. Have you eaten supper yet?"

"Oh. That's right." He'd sigh. Then we'd have the same conversation again in about twenty minutes.

The day went on, and a storm blew through. I was glad that our Jedi training was after the big storm. Yay for us, right?

Accordingly, after we ate supper at Hollywood and Vine, I took both of my Padawans by the hand, and led them to the Jedi training to suit up in their robes.

(continued)

(*continued*)

"Now? Is it time to fight Darth Vader now?" He anxiously asked.

"Almost, sweetie. Almost."

They led the kids to the stage and there we saw you, Mr. Jedi-man. You were funny, entertaining, and great with the kids.

Then, Darth Vader made a wonderfully dramatic entrance!

Omg. Here we go!

I looked at Josiah's face which was plastered with the biggest grin I'd ever seen.

My face was too.

The assisting Jedi sent kid after kid to center stage to battle the Sith Lord. My daughter, Esther, was so cute! She stood so far away from him to "fight." I laughed and enjoyed watching her.

This is so cute!

Five left . . . Now four. It began to sprinkle rain.

Three left. Now two. Now . . .

"We're sorry ladies and gentlemen. Due to the rain, the Jedi academy is closed."

Josiah stood there onstage; lightsaber at the ready. He turned and locked his eyes on mine. Then he screwed his face up and cried.

"No! Nooooo! I didn't get to!"

He ran to me and I held him while he cried.

I'm sure most people would, on observing this, assume he is spoiled. I assure you he isn't.

This is Autism. He was fixated on something, then didn't get to do it. The vacation would be ruined for him—and we were only in day two of it. Nothing we do can ever get him back on track once he derails. I began to cry despite myself. This would be all he would remember of his Disney trip.

I locked eyes with you. Do you remember? I was crying like a blubbering dummy.

I motioned for you to come to me. You stood there and looked around for a second. I motioned again. You took a hesitant step my way . . . then another. We stood face to face in the pouring rain.

"He's autistic." I choked out. "This is all he's talked about all day. Is there *anything* you can do?"

"Meet me around the side there." You nobly said. Kudos to staying in character the entire time, by the way.

We made our way around to the side of the stage, amid a sea of parents, kids, and cheery cast members.

There you were, waiting all Jedi-like in an alcove. Waiting for Josiah.

You then made a "Grand presentation" to him and gave him Darth Vader's lightsaber—autographed by the Dark Lord himself!

Say what!?

Josiah was in awe. You gave him the moon, Mr. Jedi Master. You fixed his day . . . his entire vacation! You got him back on track.

I couldn't help but cry, and I'm crying now remembering your generosity of spirit for my little boy. You easily could have thrown your hands up when I motioned for you. You could have pointed to your character handler and shrugged a fake "I'm sorry." You could have simply ignored me and turned your back.

But you didn't.

You may not even remember this moment, it was so small for you. I would be remiss, though, if I didn't fully explain how you . . . YOU, Jedi Master made a ruined moment beautiful. Thank you from the very bottom of my heart.

We spent the rest of the night jumping in puddles, riding rides, enjoying the nearly empty streets of Hollywood Studios, and watching Fantasmic.

Thank you, again. You will never know how you helped us out. To say that you made our vacation is not an exaggeration.

Most Sincerely and Appreciatively,

Sharon Kay Edwards

Source: Reproduced by permission of Sharon Kay Edwards.

If your eyes are dry reading Sharon's story, we are worried about your soul. Seriously.

The post was shared on Sharon's blog as well as the *Huffington Post*, where it received more than 1 million combined reads. Disney is no small brand. When we asked about it on Facebook and Twitter, no one replied, "What is this Disney you speak of? Never heard of it." It can be very intimidating as small business owners or employees to aspire to be like such a prolific brand—but we shouldn't let that stop us from bringing this kind of magic into our own companies. What the Jedi did that day didn't rely on big budgets or a huge team. He was kind and human, and he cared about the experience of one family in a sea of thousands. It should be easier for a small business to operate that way, not the opposite. We have a choice. We can let stories like these inspire us or let them limit us by setting up "just" statements about ourselves. Some people will read this chapter and be inspired. Others will say, "I am just one employee" or "just a small business" or "just a boring old (enter any product here) company." *UnSelling* is about choosing to aspire, rather than be just another company or employee.

13

Information

OTHER THAN THE impulse buys in line at the grocery store or the stack of DVDs I keep buying but never watch, I, like all people, make purchasing decisions based on information. The best thing about today's world of social media and online interaction is that consumers have more information than ever before. And unlike in the past, it doesn't come from only the brands themselves.

When we looked at the sales cloud, all the words inside were information sources: online reviews, social media, podcasts, blogs, and so on. These trusted referrals, along with Google, provide endless amounts of information about purchase decisions. When we talk about AutoTrader a little further on in this book, we are going to see how it uses information about cars to distinguish itself as an expert and the go-to site for anyone looking for a new car. It's this shift in information control—from the brands to the consumers—that I love most about today's online world. Access to information is the best tool for consumer advocacy.

Information doesn't affect only buying decisions; it also shapes companies and their choices.

Tom Webster, of BrandSavant.com, who you may remember from such other books as *UnMarketing* and *The Book of Business Awesome/ The Book of Business UnAwesome*, wrote a great post on his blog that shows us how we use information as companies to make decisions—for better or for worse.

> ### Open-Plan Offices Make People Unhappy
>
> That's the conclusion of this multinational study of worker satisfaction in open-plan and closed-plan offices. The study surveyed more than 40,000 employees in 303 office buildings in the United States, Finland, Australia, and Canada, and the results were clear: 58 percent of workers in low-partitioned cubicles and 59 percent of employees in high-partitioned cubicles were dissatisfied with the level of sound privacy in their workplace.
>
> What I love about this data is how it challenges the conventional wisdom that open-plan offices foster productivity. I have not seen any data that demonstrates that open plan offices do any such thing. In fact, there is plenty of other evidence to the contrary. But that isn't what interests me most about this particular study.
>
> No, what I found interesting was that the study's authors did not actually attempt to gauge productivity; they focused solely on employee satisfaction. When asked why they did not study productivity, the short answer was that it's too hard to do. Traditional productivity tests ask employees to engage in simple tasks (such as proofreading) to determine their variable level of output.
>
> What productivity measures are crap at, however, is measuring how productive you are when you engage in creative work, such as problem solving. The fact that this recent study of worker satisfaction essentially takes a pass on measuring productivity is therefore not an indictment of this survey, which is very good. Rather, it's a sign that anytime we see these sorts of studies attempt to measure productivity in noneconomic terms, it's a hand wave.
>
> And finally, I've worked in open-plan offices, closed offices, and (currently) my kitchen counter. Open-plan offices are terrible.

Who hasn't been sold on the idea that open-plan offices are better? The cubicle is practically a symbol of workplace horror. Cold, divided, each one exactly like the next, not exactly a creative wonderland! Entrepreneurs dream of the archetypical cool office space, open concept and hip.

Our decisions as consumers are based on the information we have access to and the quality of that information. In the study, the authors measured satisfaction instead of productivity. Would the results have been different if they hadn't? How can a study quantify something as unquantifiable as satisfaction anyway? The key here is that studies and data are complicated, and the results they yield can be skewed. The only case study you should be focusing on for your business is the one you are currently running—with your customers and your employees. There is a danger in changing your office or newsletter design based on a study without ever asking your employees or readers what they think.

Information guides our choices. We learn about health risks and make purchase decisions to keep our families safe. Ratings on everything from video games to seat belts, to which trips we take, to the cities we move to, are all based on information. We use analytics to improve our websites, marketing, and content. But we need to be looking closely and critically at these analytics to make sure we're making the best choices for our business.

One of the issues of looking at site analytics for things such as "most common search phrases used" is we don't see what went into getting users to search that in the first place. One of the top search terms that leads people to unmarketing.com is "unmarketing keynote" or "scott stratten keynote." Did they hear someone talking about one of my talks at an event? Were they listening to the UnPodcast or someone else's podcast? Did they read about me somewhere? We don't take into account how content marketing[1] and word of mouth fuel the search request.

I am fascinated, as you should be, by what has led people to the search itself. I've sat down and spoken with people who've booked me and asked how they found me. Recently, the answer was that a man's sister shared a clip of my QR code rant, which he watched and then searched "scott stratten keynote." He searched the term, visited my speaking site, and booked me to keynote his company's event.

---

[1] This includes blogs, articles, interviews, and so on.

From a data perspective, the booking would come up as a referral from Google. But in reality it should be classified as a referral from sister through content marketing. We give the credit to Google when the credit should be given to YouTube, Facebook, his sister, and Google. Data is great, and analytics are wonderful, but they rarely tell the whole story.

We could decide to take these analytics at face value. Load up my site content and social media posts with "Scott Stratten Keynote" and make them as keyword rich as possible. But this ignores the real meaning behind the data. The best search engine optimization (SEO) I can do is to create compelling content people want to share with others. I didn't get on stage the day I filmed the QR code rant that got their attention and think about being keyword rich; I went on and gave it my all.

14

Motivation

WE CAN'T UNDERSTAND where we're aiming without looking at the why—and that's where motivation comes in. Motivation is important because the why of each decision we make can shape every step. Some brands will never stand a chance with certain customers because of the why. Groups motivated by religious values, for example, may make purchase decisions entirely based on this why—no matter how high quality a product or service or what kind of experiences they create. They will seek out brands that support their values and disregard those that don't. Environmentally conscious companies bank on the motivation of the customers, focusing marketing on a set of shared values and expectations. Industries affected by government policies or pressures from international trade create incentives and policy to encourage companies to make certain decisions about manufacturing. Entirely new industries come to life over motivations for better health and well-being. Do you remember the gluten-free product industry from 10 years ago? Neither do I.

Here are some examples of possible customer motivations:

- I want to make a choice that corresponds with my values about health and well-being.

- I want to make a choice that will make me feel good about my spending and allow me to save money for other purchases.
- I want to make a choice that all my friends are making.

And some company motivation examples:

- We want to make a choice that will set us apart as the best product in our industry.
- We want to make a choice that will lower our costs.
- We want to make a choice that will create the least amount of changes from last year.

And some industry motivation examples:

- We want to be kind to the environment.
- We want to be known as an American manufacturing supporter.
- We want to keep our industry relevant in the face of technological change.

When customer motivations are met by the brand motivations, we have a significant reason to choose that company. One of the best ways for customers to find out what brand motivations are is through social media, because it allows for passive conversations and venting. We've learned to be very skeptical of commercials and controlled kinds of media where the company is in control of the message. Instead, in social, we see other consumers sharing their experiences and we trust those more, because they aren't being pushed at us.

And then sometimes companies get the why very, very wrong, like when Bic decided to design pens for women . . . because of course women, when deciding which writing utensil to work with, wanted one that was small enough for their dainty hands—or maybe not.

Here are two of the hundreds of Amazon product reviews:[1]

> This pen is great. I bought it for all my female friends and relatives. It enabled them, finally, to write things (although they may not yet know to do so on paper; but you can only expect so much, really). I thought they were just a bit slow.

[1]Source: http://bit.ly/UnBic

My mother, a hard-working woman who raised twelve kids single-handedly whilst doing all the ironing (as nature intended), was furtively abashed by her illiteracy. Long would she gaze upon her husband and sons' scrawlings and would dedicate five minutes a day (which she really should have spent making sandwiches) to pray that one day she would be granted the ability to create such scribbles of her own. She's still a little slow on the uptake, but this product has definitely helped start the ball rolling. We tried to give her men's pens but she used to rip the cartridges out and drink the ink. Typical woman.

Anyway, it's good that BIC are finally doing something to aid the plight of women. Hopefully a range of 'for her' paperclips is on the horizon—my wife has an awful time keeping her recipes together.

And

My boyfriend never usually buys me gifts. I mean, the pleasure of his company is more than enough for me, I am told. So imagine my surprise when, one valentine's day morning, I awoke to find a beautiful purple box perched on my pillow! Well, I LOVE the colour purple, so you can imagine my overwhelming joy at receiving such a gift! My trembling, perfectly manicured and weak fingers were ineffective at opening the box, so you can imagine the building excitement I endured waiting for my boyfriend to get home and open it for me.

Well let me tell you it was worth the wait! The soft grip, feminine colour and lightweight material finally allowed me to experience something I had only dreamed of, as I would watch countless men in a graceful and effortless show of gliding pen on paper. Although MY markings can do little more than make the "X" I use to sign my name, I feel like I'm part of some strange

(continued)

(*continued*)
new world, full of possibilities! I feel I can be anything I want, like . . . a waitress. . . .

But I dream.

For now, I use my downtime between looking pretty and laughing at my boyfriend's jokes to practise my craft, and one day show the world what women can do when they put their mind to it. Dare to think big, girls! Our time has come.

But they really need more sparkles. And if only the ink was more feminine. maybe pink or purple or even pale green. And maybe the ink could sparkle too? So I'd feel like a princess when I write?

But really, whatever the men at Bic think is best. I'm sure they know what I need.

There are many, many more like these. Why would a person buy a Bic pen for women? Well, first of all they would need to be having serious lady issues with the usual pens already available. Clearly, they were not.

Businesses are meant to solve pain points for customers, to meet needs. As the world changes, needs change and motivation leads to creation. This year at the Consumer Electronics Show (CES) there was no less than an entire building dedicated to phone chargers and cases, a need that did not exist years ago. Wearable technology was everywhere: fitness and sport training equipment and technologies aimed at improving the lives of an aging population, such as monitors that measure heart rate, pulse, weight, and even glucose levels for people with diabetes. Allowances in our house are already being saved for Oculus Rift, a virtual reality gaming headset. Because they need to have them—that's why.

Answering the why for our customers and clients is our main job. Our motivations for our business need to put customers first. When was the last time you asked yourself why you're in business? If one of the answers isn't to meet the needs of your market, you don't need to look any further into why sales have been dropping lately. If you aren't answering a why, you don't get to blame social media, marketing, or online shopping for your lack of customers. New whys are always coming forward; that's why keeping an eye and ear on the pulse of your market is so important. That way, when new questions come forward, you can be there to answer them.

15

Why Boston Will Have Fewer Check-Ins

WE'VE ALREADY SEEN some great examples of how there is no such thing as a neutral brand interaction and how each pulse point is an opportunity to create a great, shareable experience. Some examples are straightforward: We get a bad product or experience bad service, and we move on to a competitor's brand and post on Facebook about the whole thing. Here the line between an external factor such as horrible coffee and the pulse reaction of changing coffee shops is clear and straight. But what about when the pulse point is less clear?

The 2014 running of the Boston Marathon was historic. One year after bombs exploded near the finish line, killing three and injuring more than 200, the city and the world were behind the athletes like never before. Determination and a refusal to let the tragedy of 2013 stop them was felt everywhere. Images of the crowd and runners filled social media, television, and newspapers. You couldn't help but feel inspired by the marathon.

The excitement led to a lot of runners, and fans, wanting to be a part of the day. To qualify you had to run the qualifying time, be at least 18, and sign up by the deadline. People train and prepare for years to be a part of it. There is a pride to wearing one of those bibs and crossing the finish line, as there should be. So when it started coming out that some runners who hadn't qualified or signed up in time to earn theirs had decided to run with fake ones, the reaction was deservedly negative. This would have been true any year, and when you add in the additional symbolism for this year's race, the reaction was downright, across the board outrage.

Foursquare chief executive officer (CEO) Dennis Crowley was not one of these fakers. He ran the race legitimately, after not being able to complete it in 2013. Unfortunately, he ran the race with his wife, who was accused after the race as running as a bandit, the term for someone who races without registering or paying any fees and using someone else's number. Crowley had even gone so far as to "put her Twitter handle on the bib, and had tweeted about running as a bandit."[1] The true bib owner found out about the fake after searching for pictures of herself running using her number and found images of another woman, Crowley.

The Crowleys issued the following apology:

> Hey all -
>
> Dennis Crowley (Chelsa's husband) here chiming in on this. First of all, our apologies to anyone we offended. After running together last year, getting split up and not finishing together (Chelsa finished, I did not), we both felt like we needed to run again and finish together to get closure. I wrote a blog post about our experiences last year and my motivation to run Boston again this year: https://medium.com/editors-pic.
>
> Yes, using a duplicate number to get Chelsa into the starting corral with me was wrong. I don't expect everyone to understand our strong need to run and and [sic] finish together—but after trying unsuccessfully to get a charity number and trying unsuccessfully to officially transfer a number from an injured-runner
>
> *(continued)*

---

[1]Source: http://bit.ly/BostonFoursquare

(*continued*)
friend, we did what we could to make sure we could run together in hopes of finishing together.

I sent an email to Kathy Brown, the woman who rightfully earned #34033 to apologize for any disrespect, hurt feelings or confusion. Our intent was never to "steal" anything from anyone—our intent was to finish the Boston Marathon together as we tried to do last year. (#34033 = first 3 numbers of my number + "33" which is Chelsa's age. We chose a number close to my number to ensure we'd be next to each other at the start.)

Again, sincerest apologies to anyone we offended or disrespected, including the BAA and the police/fire/EMT crews that worked so hard to make sure Monday's race was safe for all runners.

Dennis + Chelsa

I learned about the controversy on Facebook, where it was spreading like crazy. Friends who had qualified and run the marathon were furious. Everyone who had run the race in 2013, the spectators, the city, the country, and the world who had watched had all been affected by the events of the day. But using those events as an excuse to be fraudulent and negate the hard work of those who had earned those bibs was simply unacceptable.

As the story spread, more and more the link was attached to a statement of anger against Foursquare. People were deleting their accounts. It seemed that faking out a spot at the 2014 Boston Marathon was a brand interaction that drove the pulse into the ground. We're going to talk more about these kinds of indirect and direct offenses a little later in this book. The line here between pulse point interaction and the change in people's usage decisions may be a little less straightforward but no less true. Losing customers because the CEO and his wife offended the public is no less related than if they'd closed their accounts because of bad service. A pulse point is any interaction as defined by the customer and/or market. It's not up to Dennis and Chelsa whether or not they were making a brand statement that day—the market is making that decision for them.

16

Brand Flatline

It's Not Me; It's You.

SOMETIMES, WE JUST need to let a brand go. And there is no going back.

The offense too offensive, the service too poor, the product causing more problems than it could ever solve. The pulse goes flat, and there is no way to get the relationship going again.

It's not me, horrible company; it's you.

Flatlines are opportunities for competition. One of the reasons to be active in listening to conversations online about not only your company but your competitors is to catch the flatlines. We see flatlines online more than the bumps along the way because they're extreme—and that's what gets shared online more than anything else. We're all much more interested in the worst burger you've ever had in your entire life that made you throw up than we are in the burger that could have been a little hotter. That's just humans.

I've stayed in a ton of hotels. Some were outstanding; some I will continue to go back to over and over. Many needed a few improvements, but mostly did the trick. I'd go back. A few were bad: uncomfortable bed, cold and old room service (not a good combination for anything in life), and customer service staff who were rude and unhelpful. I'd never go back to those. But I've only ever left one, once.

Here is my TripAdvisor review of that gem of a hotel.

"Worst Decision of My Life." Reviewed 8 February 2013

I travel for a living. I've also lead a colorful life and have been in some pretty bad places. Econo Lodge Jersey City wins for:

1. Most I've ever been scared.
2. Worst hotel room.
3. Worst front desk person.
4. Worst front desk person behind glass.
5. Most avoided by taxis.
6. Most frequent drug deals out front.
7. Quickest hotel stay (3.5 mins in room, 2 hours out front waiting for a cab).

I made the mistake of booking here based on the Econo Lodge brand because of a last minute change and I had to go to Hoboken the next day and all the other hotels were full. Sleeping in the turnpike would have been safer.

Never. Ever stay here.

Room Tip: "The rooms on the ground floor are easier to see the drug deals out front"

That is a brand flatline. When a tired traveller waits 2 hours for a taxi rather than sleep in your hotel, that is not a social media problem. This is not a TripAdvisor problem.

The manager of Econo Lodge replied to my review.

Dear Stratola,

I am writing to thank you for taking the time to post your stay experience review at our hotel.

I would like to apologize for failing to exceed your expectations. Your satisfaction is important to us and we will be using the feedback you provided to make improvements to ensure we offer an outstanding experience to our guests in the future.

Hope that you will consider staying with us again so that we can have another chance to provide you with a better experience.

Sincerely,

Manager

Econo Lodge

This type of apology was on every review left for this sorry excuse for a hotel. This is a prime example of trying to put icing on a crap cake. No amount of attentiveness or cut-and-paste apologies can change the fact that this is a horrible property.

The most valuable quality of social media is our ability as brands to listen to the passive conversations of our market. I've said many times on stage that if I'd come to brands 15 years ago with a tool that allowed us to listen in on casual conversations between potential customers that they would have offered me a million dollars to sign up. But now that social media is here, and is free, everyone wants to know what the return on investment (ROI) is? Flatlines are opportunities for competitors. The first thing companies need to do in social is set up listening tools for terms related to their industry. Even from this one flatline story, a competitor could have learned some valuable information about what customers are looking for:

1. Safe, clean hotels > dirty, dangerous hotels.
2. Jersey City hotels, the Econo Lodge is losing customers, do you have rooms available?
3. Taxi drivers, if you are willing to risk it, there may be some good tippers waiting for rides out of the Econo Lodge.
4. Check in to your own hotel and see what the front desk person is like. If he or she is rude, that's the first, and possibly last, impression you will ever get to make.

Econo Lodge, you're dead to me.

17

Avoid the Brand Attack

MORE THAN ANY other advice businesses ask for help with is how to avoid the attack—the outrage. That is, how can they keep from being Internet famous—and not for their new viral video. Early detection of a brand attack is all about keeping your ear on the pulse of your customers.

I love New York City. After Las Vegas, it is our favorite place in the world. Chelsea Market, Broadway, Shake Shack, Carnegie Deli. I consider the place a home away from home. The problem with New York being a home away from home is that I need to get there. And as much as I love the city, I hate their airports: JFK, LaGuardia, and Newark, the three horsemen of the travel apocalypse. Newark has gotten slightly better in the past few years . . . but anyway.

So when I found myself in line at JFK security during the dance of the flight attendants, you can guess I wasn't exactly surprised. We got to the airport early, as good Canadians do, and were in line watching other travelers step ahead of us in line because they were late. We get it; you need to make your flight. Who would have thought there'd be traffic in NEW YORK CITY?

Finally, we got to the front of the line and got naked, and I proceeded to push my bucket through the x-ray machine when the dance of the flight attendants began. Have you ever been in line when this happens? I know they need to make it to the plane in time. But the thing is, I also know the first rule of flight club: The plane won't take off without them. It will, however, leave without me. One after the other, they throw their buckets ahead of mine, pushing and elbowing, until my Canadian politeness cannot hold me, and I reach level nine Canadian anger: swearing.

"Come on![1] Not even one excuse me?"

I think I may have added a "sorry" on to the end, just to represent my country.

The last attendant heard me and turned around angrily. *Delta* shining off her lapel, she shot me an angry, dismissive look and said, "I said excuse me. If you didn't hear me, why don't you open your ears?"

I was beside myself. My mama taught me right. I don't care where you come from, how much money you make, or what kind of job you do; that does not excuse you from common courtesy. By the time I was through security, I was speechless. Have you ever been so angry at a brand that you start making a shun list? I would never fly Delta again. My son would never fly Delta again. His unborn children would never fly Delta. If they wanted to make it up to me, I would need my own plane. Delta would be changed to Scott. I wanted to sit on the captain's lap. And I wanted two bags of peanuts when I asked for them, without a saucy look from anyone when I asked. I did the only thing a self-entitled social media big deal can do: I tweeted.

Scott Stratten
@unmarketing

Detla airlines flight attendant pushes in front of me at JFK security, when asked for at least an "excuse me" she replies "open your ears"

I was so furious, I was so blind with anger, I misspelled *Delta*. Did you see it? I didn't either. Two groups of people you need to be listening to in your social media management system: angry misspellers and the all-cappers.

---

[1] Yes, that is Canadian swearing.

Within 3 minutes, I received this reply from Delta airlines.

Delta Assist
@DeltaAssist

@unmarketing I'm truly sorry to hear this.
We expect our Flight Attendants to
be courteous at all times. Please accept my
apology.   ^LH

It seems they have so many blind, angry misspellings of their name that they have a search set up for them. That's some effective social media strategizing right there! The response totally disarmed me. I went from being a raging misspeller to a calm airline traveller in 140 characters or less. I wasn't offered anything for free. I was simply treated with respect and had my frustration acknowledged and apologized for.

Scott Stratten
@unmarketing

@DeltaAssist well that made me smile.
Thank-you :) You just diffused my anger.

Immediacy is one of the most important thing in social media response. We speak a lot about authenticity and appropriateness, but without immediacy your message will be lost and ineffective. Early response is the best way to prevent a brand attack.

If this reply had been sent 3 hours later, I would have been angrily stewing on the plane, every tiny interaction with the staff fueling my frustration. The conversation online would have continued without me sharing their reply.

What about if it had been sent three days or even three weeks later?

In 20 minutes I went from irate to smiling. Then when I got on the flight, the person serving drinks was one of the nicest people I've dealt with, and no she didn't know it was me. She was just wonderful with everyone.

When it hits the fan, it's not time to hide behind the fan; it's time to be awesome.

The speed with which we reply to things exponentially changes the response. When people complain on Twitter, they are looking for validation and an apology. They want respect, courtesy, and immediacy.

Many say there is no ROI in social media, and I agree. There's ROI in being responsive and awesome and sometimes that happens in social media. I've heard a lot of brands say they don't want to use social media because they're afraid of negative interactions. That doesn't make any sense. The negative brand sentiment doesn't vanish because you're not there to be a part of it. It just gets unheard, and the anger brews.

The tool doesn't solve the problem. If your product or service sucks, it is just going to suck harder in social. But when used right, it can be a tool for amazing customer service, sending customers back into the sales cloud with great stories to share.

18

The Three Types of Pulse
We Need to Pay Attention To

WE JUST SPENT a whole lot of book talking about pulse and how an individual's experience with a brand is never neutral—but always changing—and how external and internal factors and AIM shape that pulse line.

In the next section of this book, we are going to look at three kinds of pulse: industry pulse, company pulse, and customer pulse.

For industry pulse, we are going to talk about the video game industry and Ubisoft. In an industry that is changing at lightning speed, how can a company keep up and be successful?

Taking the pulse of your industry means looking at factors such as technology changes and advancements, laws and regulations, and trends.

For company pulse, I am going to share with you some of the challenges and changes we've faced over the years at UnMarketing.

As an entrepreneur with a growing company, it's important to keep an eye inward.

For customer pulse, we are going to look to one of my perfect *UnSelling* examples: Big Ass Fans. Really, these guys could be an example for every section, but we are going to look at how, by staying connected with their community, they have created a profitable company while treating people with respect.

19

The Game of Loyalty

I HAVE NO problem admitting I'm a geek—was one before it was cool to be one. I grew up collecting comics, promising myself that when I became successful I'd buy all the incredible statues of my favorite characters that were outside the reach of my kid-sized budget. Fast-forward to today and my coworkers are Rhino, Wolverine, and the Joker, to name three of the 40 I own. Like I said, I'm a geek ☺

Along with comic books, video games have been a part of my life since Atari 2600. So when Toronto's Fan Expo[1] was announced, combining video games and comic books, we packed up the family, bought our VIP early access passes, and headed into the city.

Our passes meant that we were in the first group of people into the convention, so when we arrived, some booths were still working on setting up. The kids wanted to try the demos of the new games that were coming out,[2] so we hurried passed the other VIPs, most of whom were in costume, toward the video game section. If you don't hit those

---

[1]When originally typing this on a flight, I wrote "Fax Expo" and snort-laughed on the plane. I may be on the TSA watch list now.
[2]And by kids, I mean me and the kids. I feel sorry for Alison sometimes . . . a lot of the time.

games early, the line-ups turn Disneyworld-sized, and I didn't want to miss my, I mean the kids', chance to play.

My son tried out Ubisoft's latest installment of Splinter Cell, which was cool since being a Halo/Call of Duty household, we'd never really gotten into the series. He really enjoyed the demo and played for as long as he could. Since the game just came out and this was the big launch, we decided to buy a copy. Well played, marketing people! Played demo; bought game. Ta-da!

We walked over to the checkout counter in the game area, where two people were frantically running around, trying to figure something out. Turns out, the cash register wasn't booting up properly, so they couldn't process any sales. I know a lot of you can feel the agony right now. You've done everything right and all you have to do is take their money, and boom. Nothing.

For the record, I was being surprisingly calm and patient. I didn't even threaten to tweet! Then one of the guys behind the counter let us know he was waiting on a fix. Although he was from Ubisoft and not EB games, who were the ones doing sales at the show, he promised to do everything possible to make sure we got the game.

Did I mention it was my son's birthday?

We watched the line grow and shrink as people tried to buy games and merchandize and then bailed on their purchases when they realized the registers weren't working. With time to kill, we got to talking to our new Ubisoft friend. He stood and chatted with the kids and us, taking an actual interest in what we were saying, even with the chaos around him. At a certain moment, he finally decided we'd waited long enough and walked us over to one of the bigger EB Games displays on the other side of the gaming area. He took us to the front of the line and let the sales staff know that this family would like to purchase a game and to please help them immediately. He stayed with us the whole time to make sure all went well. On top of this, he said if we were ever in Montreal, that we could do a tour of their studios and gave us his card. Turned out he was Robert Donsky, Sales Director for Canada at Ubisoft!

Robert was in charge of the national rollout of Ubisoft's biggest title that quarter, and he spent almost 20 minutes with us on the purchase of one copy. One. He had no idea who I was or what I do for a living. Nothing. He simply made it his mission to ensure my son got his birthday present, and we left the booth happy.

Ubisoft went from a gaming studio I'd heard of but didn't pay much attention to, to my front-of-mind brand. I started seeing the logo everywhere. It wasn't that that the logo hadn't been everywhere before; I just never noticed it. The experience changed my brain about the brand. Robert changed the meaning of Ubisoft's logo. Once we noticed the logo, we started looking at other game titles and realized Ubisoft was the company that developed the Prince of Persia game series, one I played religiously. We bought a bunch of others to try out. In a room full of video game titles and companies competing for our attention, Ubisoft won out.

We ended up talking about Robert on the UnPodcast and sharing the story of how we met. We e-mailed him and let him know when we'd be in Montreal because I was keynoting a conference in the city. He was floored we were talking about him and grateful for the unexpected promotion. We arranged a tour and ended up doing a talk with their sales/marketing team over lunch. The tour was fantastic, and our boys were in heaven.

Every potential/current customer you run into is impressionable. Your brand is never static; you change it with every interaction, good or bad. No matter what your position is with a company, whether you sell wholesale to Walmart, or products one by one in a storefront, you are always making an impression. In 2001, Ubisoft Canada was ranked 16; today it is the third largest publisher in the world. As Ubisoft has grown over the past 13 years, so have its brands. Assassins Creed, Rabbids, Just Dance, and the Tom Clancy franchise are now world-renown brands. No doubt, some of the company's success can be tied back to employees like Robert.

When we asked Robert how the video game industry had changed and Ubisoft's place within that change, here is what he had to say:

> Boy, oh boy, has the industry changed. Going back to when I first started, I was selling games like Myst, Chessmaster, and Rayman on PC. PC gaming was still king, and online gaming was still just a blip. And then it happened! PS2, GameCube, and the long-awaited Xbox launched, and everything changed. The first major game I sold was Splinter Cell on the original Xbox, and that changed Ubisoft forever. It is literally what put us on the map. Gaming was becoming

more accessible with the new consoles, the experience and graphics were getting better, and playing online was now easy with platforms like Xbox live. The gaming industry was also becoming more competitive as more and more independent publishers were popping up, which in turn forced everyone to make better games! We (the sales team) used to sell games; now our clients WANT our games.

That is exactly what *UnSelling* is all about: creating great products, offering support when needed, and having people like Robert, who take the time to care about each and every customer, out there creating ecstatic customers.

We also asked Robert about customer feedback and how Ubisoft uses this information to improve the company:

> I take customer feedback very seriously. Doesn't matter if it's an 11-year-old kid or one of our major clients. Everyone is important. Whenever I receive feedback, I try my best to pass the information along to the right department. I have to admit, I have a soft spot for kids. Over the years, I have received a few letters where a consumer got a busted game or something didn't work properly. I would always send out a nice care package to ensure we are providing the best customer service.

We can certainly vouch for Robert on this one. He was wonderful with our kids and treated them with kindness and respect at the show and later during our tour. What is the value of one 12-year-old kid on his birthday? The sale of one game, the happiness of his parent, bringing notice to your brand, and creating awareness and loyalty.

Robert feels the environment at Ubisoft is the reason the company has been so successful:

> I have to say the work environment at Ubisoft is unparalleled to anything I have seen personally. First and foremost, we work in an open environment, which I feel is a huge benefit. As sales director, it allowed me to work closely with my team and keep an open communication and share ideas. It's important nowadays to have an inviting work environment for employees. At Ubisoft, we are fortunate to have an

in-house doctor, a gym, a massage therapist, a rooftop terrace over the studio, excellent medical benefits, and the list goes on. Ubisoft offers services that make employees important.

Attracting and keeping great employees should be the job of every company. Ubisoft didn't set out to create a story to be shared on social media. It didn't craft a message, push it out, and try to bribe bloggers to talk about the company. Its people were just awesome, and them being that way was shared.

And last, we asked Robert what he hoped people thought of when they see or hear Ubisoft's name:

> I would hope they think of a major player, not only in the gaming industry, but as player in the entertainment industry—a company that is at the forefront of technology and is always trying to innovate. It wouldn't hurt if they think that Ubisoft makes kick-ass games as well!

When I think of Ubisoft, I think of amazing customer service and a company that took time to make a birthday kid's day. To me, that's what branding and *UnSelling* are really about: taking the time and making the effort to create an experience for every customer, not only the big ones, or the important ones, but each and every one.

20

What Really Matters in Branding

IN BUSINESS AND marketing, we spend a lot of time, and money, on logos. If you've ever worked on a logo design, you know exactly what I mean. And if it was a rebranding design, then take all that money, time, and effort and double it. *Rebranding* is really French for "spend ridiculous amounts of money and time you'll never, ever, ever get back."

We opened *UnSelling* with a story about the Ritz-Carlton and Joshie. When people think about logos, this is what they think about:

THE RITZ-CARLTON

It's so fancy, isn't it? If you've worked on a logo design, you can probably imagine the weeks or months spent on this. There was a right-facing lion camp, a left-facing lion camp, a conservative, tongue-in camp. And there was an entire subcommittee font argument that took place. Some weird guy in the corner talking about Comic Sans . . .

You know who should design logos? Designers. I've seen people who can't even put an outfit together in the morning giving input on logos. Hire experts, and let them do their jobs.

A logo is meant to do two things. If you don't know the brand, it should give you some idea of what the company is all about. I assume from this one that the Ritz-Carlton is a very fancy, royal lion-like place. If you know the brand, the logo will remind you of the most extreme and the most recent experience you had with them. This is the Ritz-Carlton to me:

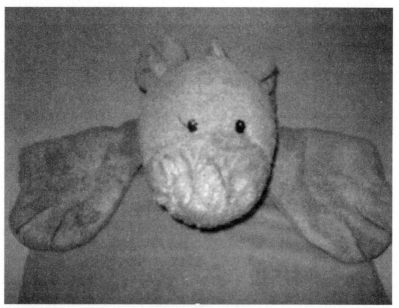

Source: Reproduced by permission of Chris Hurn.

Joshie. That's what I think of when I think of the hotel brand: Joshie and how wonderful it was to stay at the resort personally.

In 2014, the company Blacks underwent a rebrand. The brand repicturing included a new logo, an app for photo printing, a website, and new store designs. Photography is one of the industries that has undergone huge transformation with new technologies over the past few years. It would be hard to find an industry that has changed more. Today, everyone has a high-resolution camera in their pockets, connected to sharing platforms that link them to friends and family and the world. Everything from life stages and events, to important moments and achievements, to the food we have for lunch are photographed, posted, and shared in minutes. So a business concept that relies on people going into a mall to have their images printed is one that certainly needs a "repicturing" . . . and then some.

We do still print out pictures. I know I do. I print them for my mom, or for the house, or sometimes as gifts. We were recently at the Eaton Centre in Toronto and wanted to print out a picture for my sister who just had a baby. We bought a frame and saw there was a Blacks in the mall. Perfect! Business coming your way, printing store!

I had the photo on my phone, so I figured it would be as easy as connecting to the store's printers and watching the photo magic happen. When we got the store, an employee let us know that we could use Blacks' new app to upload the image, since all the computers in the location were being used. I do love when an app makes things easier and hate waiting in line, so I happily got the app and found my niece's picture for printing. Once everything was ready to go, I used the app to send the photo for printing and waited. I assumed the wait time would be a few minutes, time enough for the magic of technology to do its work. I asked a salesperson how long we'd be waiting, and she let me know I could come back in a few hours.

A few hours? But the printers are right there.

I could literally have driven home from Toronto, sent the image from my desktop to my local Walmart, and picked it up faster.

I assumed she was making some kind of mistake. "It takes a few hours? But I installed your app and sent the image in already. Why does it take a few hours?" I asked her, as patiently as possible.

Irritated by the question, she let me know that "as a customer courtesy, she would be able to get my picture printed for me in about an hour."

A customer courtesy?

I was speechless. Did she know, I wondered, that they have printers in homes now that print high-resolution images in just minutes? Why would anyone choose to use this service when so many other options were faster and of equal quality? I wondered whether she considered using other words than *customer courtesy* when answering me and watched Alison make her "he'll make you famous if you say something like that again" face.

Needless to say, we left the store without the picture.

Having an app doesn't make a company tech savvy and modern if it doesn't improve service. It won't matter what the new logo looks like or how cool the new store locations are if a company ignores the basic changes in its industry that are keeping customers from using its services. To get people to leave their homes and print out their photos will take more than a fresh coat of brand paint; it's going to take something new, the answer to a new why.

What matters in branding is what you do. Your brand isn't what you say it is; it's what your customers experience and tell others. You can craft a professional image, dress it up in expensive design, and send it out into the world, but if it comes with stories that don't match, the stories will win every single time.

21

The Pulse of an UnAwesome Industry

"SURE, SCOTT, UBISOFT can be do amazing things in its industry because video games are cool! But in my industry (enter any other industry . . . ever), we have rules and standards and guidelines that keep us from using Twitter/Facebook/blogs. How can we make great choices and take the pulse of our industry when the pulse is soooooo serious?"

Industry factors that affect company decisions can include everything from professional standards (licenses and accreditation) to trends, competitors, and new developments in technology. It always seems to people that their industry is the most rigid. This year alone, I was lucky enough to travel around the world, speaking to groups from a wide range of industries, from hospitality, to real estate, to investment and money management, to retail and franchising. Every one comes with its own unique pros and cons when it comes to social media and all forms of communication with their markets.

Sometimes, being part of a seemingly rigid industry encourages companies to do amazing things, creating experiences that are adored by customers and that help grow their businesses and shape their brands for the better. Other times, the industry becomes an excuse, for bad service, for bad experiences, and sometimes for not even trying. I couldn't even count how many times an audience member has dismissed the opportunities for community building online with an industry excuse: "Well, Scott, I can't possibly write a blog. In investment and wealth management there are just too many rules and issues of confidentiality."

Your industry should never be an excuse for not being awesome. In fact, working in that environment just means your good work will stand out even more. Some of my favorite social accounts belong to police departments, an industry that could not be held to higher standards.

According to Mashable, a 2013 social media survey from the International Association of Chiefs of Police found that 96 percent of police departments use social media in some capacity, and more than 80 percent say it has helped them solve crimes. Three-quarters of those on social media have joined since 2010.

Facebook is the most popular platform for police departments, with more than 92 percent of socially active departments using it. Twitter is next in line, with almost 65 percent, and almost 43 percent are on YouTube. Although it's not as widely adopted as the more traditional social platforms.

In Toronto, our local police department has a page listing all departments and individuals participating in social media with links to their pages as an extension of the communication with the community.[1] Police are also using a tool called Nextdoor.com,[2] which is like a modern-day neighborhood watch and community development platform. It's a kind of hyperlocal Facebook, where neighbors can connect privately and ask questions, look for recommendations, and just, well, be neighborly.

Police departments are using social media to extend community response to disasters, find missing people, solve crimes, answer community member questions, and listen.

Did all of that sound like an excuse to you?

To show you what I mean, here is one of my favorite examples of a police department doing social and being amazing at it.

---

[1] Source: www.torontopolice.on.ca/socialmedia/
[2] Source: http://bit.ly/PoliceSocial

Sunith Baheerathan @Sunith_DB8R
Any dealers in Vaughan wanna make a 20sac chop? Come to Keele/Langstaff Mr. Lube, need a spliff or two to help me last this open to close.
Details

 York Regional Police
@YRP

Awesome! Can we come too? MT @Sunith_DB8R Any dealers in Vaughan wanna make a 20sac chop? Come to Keele/Langstaff Mr. Lube, need a spliff.

I honestly didn't know what any of those words meant when I first read them, so I put it through an online moron translator and found out that Sunith wanted to buy some pot. He thought it smart to share this on Twitter, along with his location, which also happened to be his place of employment. Well, at the time it was anyway.

Sunith was fired. The drug buying stopped. And the news that the police were, in fact, listening on Twitter—and have a sense of humor about it—was shared. This is a perfect example of how to use Twitter effectively. They were listening, the response was timely, and the execution was perfect. The account @YRP is one of our favorites at UnMarketing, so if you're reading this, let them know we say hi.

22

Flying the Kite of Community

SITTING AROUND THE boardroom table at Kitestring Creative is a great way to spend a morning. We are lucky to have these guys as our creative team—having designed our websites, stickers, and posters for all three previous books, the Noooooooooooooooo.com app, and many of the visuals you see in talks and in this book, including pulse, pivot, and the sales cloud.

Kitestring founders, Jenn Hudder and Chris Farias,[1] are so wonderful to work with, and when watching them work together, you never want to leave the place. They have the kind of chemistry entrepreneurs hope for in a partner, and it comes to life in everything they do.

The agency's main focus areas are strategic branding, creation of integrated campaigns, and digital engagement through cutting-edge technology and responsive design. Kitestring creates brands that "move past a look and feel to become living embodiments of your company's most inspiring attributes. The narrative structure of each brand tells a story, which combines with colour and shape to develop an immersive experience for your audience."

---

[1]We were lucky enough to have Chris as a guest on the Vegas 30 podcast. You can watch/listen by going here http://bit.ly/Vegas30Chris

Aside from how silly talented they are, Kitestring is known as a strong and supportive member of its local community in Hamilton, Ontario. Neither founder is from Hamilton originally, but both grew up in small towns and missed the community feeling when they set up shop in Hamilton. They didn't know any of their neighbors when they first got started, and they wanted that to change.

Within a few months of opening their doors, the local paper landed on their doorstep with the headline "Recession," and they knew they'd need to get creative if they were going to make it.

They decided to give Twitter a try and used the site to connect to other community members.

Chris is the awesome behind the @Kitestring account. He is a perfect example of how to bring a face to your brand with personality, fun, and kindness online. In talking to him, he let us know that he once tested using their logo as their Twitter picture for a few weeks and noticed a huge drop in replies. People don't connect with faceless brands. And it's a whole lot easier to be negative with a logo than it is with a face.

Kitestring volunteers on boards for local organizations and donates time and talents to local not-for-profits. A week doesn't go by that I don't see them out at a local school or city hall teaching classes. They held the first tweet up, TEDx conference, and social media all-day workshop in Hamilton.

"We just didn't want to have to get into a car and drive to Toronto every time we wanted to do something. Of course, looking back, it would have been a lot less work just to get into the car . . . but a whole lot less rewarding."

Many of their clients are also from Hamilton, with markets in Hamilton, so being a part of the community means they have a pulse on what the community cares about and wants. *UnSelling* means understanding the value of being a part of the daily lives of those who work for you, sell to you, and buy from you.

As they told me, they believe that "if you love your city, the city [will] love you back."

At Kitestring, caring about the community isn't a policy; they attract and hire people who think along those lines. Their social media guidelines are simply "you gotta be nice" and "no swearing."

When they started out, the design industry was on the cusp of something different, and they landed on social media and did it well. Although they don't manage social media for others, they act as a perfect example of how to do it right. One of my favorite things they teach, and aim for in all their work, is that whatever they do it has to "have ripples." Ten years ago, you didn't need to think about the ripple; you could just design and sell billboards and walk out. Now things have to carry on, and that can be the most challenging part of any campaign.

They aim to bring online and offline together so that they can "dance together and amplify." As they told me, "you need to fix what's in here—before I can take it out there."

One of the campaigns Kitestring is most proud of, and that gives you an example of the founders' understanding of community, is the one they created for the YMCA of Hamilton:

In nearly every North American community, alongside the church, the high school, and the bank, you will find a YMCA. These institutions, as part of the average community landscape, fade into the background and are often taken for granted.

Fighting against the dated "swim & gym" perception has been a challenge for many YMCAs, including the YMCA of Hamilton, Burlington, and Brantford.

The YMCAHBB is doing great work, aimed at targeting the root cause of social issues such as battling poverty through education, unemployment through training, and support for newcomers and obesity through their financial assistance and mobile YMCA programming. However, their diversity of work meant too many voices, with too many messages. This regional YMCA was struggling to stay top of mind, although their community services were playing a vital role in the community. The challenge was to build a strategic theme that would bridge the communications gap between numerous service departments, locations, and audiences spread across a large geographical area.

The theme is "*Y. We are here*" solves these issues in a multifaceted way, which is how we like to work. First, it reminds the audience that the YMCA is still your neighbor and you likely already have some connection to the organization.

Second, it is used as a thematic device that allows each YMCAHBB service to speak about its own programming as the YMCAHBB's reason for existing.

These Y statements allow each part of the organization to speak in an intelligent and impactful way while staying on message.

By speaking to the benefit of the programming and answering the question *Y. We are here* as opposed to just program name-dropping (e.g., "Because our kids are tomorrow's leaders" instead of "We have camp"), it reminds the audience that they may think "swim & gym" but what the YMCAHBB delivers its communities is local results.

That has got to be one of the best campaign themes I've ever heard: Y we are here. It really shows a respect for the history of its clients and an understanding for the pulse of its customers.

23

Taking My Pulse

I WOULD REALLY love for this chapter to be all about how I took the pulse of my business and industry and reacted with foresight and intuition. But the reality is, I didn't. I would like to tell you how I shifted from making viral video slideshows for clients to social media expert because I saw it all coming—but in reality, I just had nothing else to do.

You see, when the recession hit, the market for $10,000 slideshows ceased to exist.[1] Add to the economic downturn advances in technology that put moviemaking in everyone's hand, and we were replaced. I found myself back at square one, working to rebuild my business.

I should be the case study for what happens when you don't take the pulse of your customer, company, and industry. Each of our client videos was a one-off transaction. We never looked to expand our services or even cared where the videos were going. I was content to sit back and create high-margin slideshows for eternity—to the point that I never

---

[1] Yes, the need for these amazingly existed before then.

marketed myself in any way. All new business came from referrals and word of mouth—and then the mouths stopped moving.

I remember sitting there, trying to think of what I was going to do. You can't have an agency without any clients, and I'd created no brand awareness. I was tired of being in the background, creating success for others with no link back to me. All that frustration left me burnt out and needing a place to recharge my batteries and talk to other business owners going through the same things. That's the real reason I joined Twitter. As I mentioned in *UnMarketing*, I didn't join Twitter to become an expert in it or to be called an influencer or even to get a book deal. I joined it to find what I hadn't had in years, a connection with my peers. This is why I am so defensive of how people use the platform, because I am living proof that community can overcome anything. And when all you do on Twitter is schedule and automate, you devalue and steal from the community.

The time I gave to Twitter initially was a huge leap of faith, especially without revenue coming in. I had to justify to myself, my family, and my employees that something good would come out of all the time I was investing on the site. In that moment, I wasn't sure what would come out of it, but I believed that if I put community before commerce, I could create something new and extraordinary. Turns out, it worked. You wouldn't be reading this if it hadn't. Like anything successful in business, it took timing, luck, a ton of work, and a half-cup of skill. Slowly, business started coming to me, asking for guidance through the new social media landscape. I started getting requests to speak about the subject, which is my true passion and skill set. Then came the book deal.

In 2010 *UnMarketing* was released followed by a 30-city, 10-week book tour, solely created through Twitter. I found myself at another crossroad. But this time I did take the pulse, mainly my own, which if you're an entrepreneur, you rarely take. I was speaking numerous times a month while trying to build a consulting business and sell a book. I realized quickly that if I succeeded at everything I was working toward, I would burn out. I knew I couldn't risk starting from scratch again, leaving no time for my family.

So I decided to stop offering consulting and focus solely on speaking and writing—and I've never looked back. Funny thing, as soon as I stopped consulting, more and more brands asked me to consult. It's like the person in school who became undatable and therefore suddenly so much more appealing—or deep-fried Oreos locked in a glass case: You want it a little extra because you can't have it. I was offered jobs and Fortune 500 clients. But I knew that if I wanted to be happy, I needed to stick to my decision . . . no matter how hard it was to turn down guaranteed money, especially when a year prior no money was coming in at all.

As a side note to this, taking your own pulse isn't just about what you want to do. It's also about what you can make a living doing. It's very rare for anyone to make a living doing only keynote talks at conferences and selling books. Most people speak to get consulting clients or for a nominal fee as a way to get publicity for their company. I had to make the jump from taking any gig to taking only paid ones. Just because you want to be paid to speak doesn't mean you will be paid to speak. I've also always wanted to be paid to play baseball or sing lead in a band, but through years of research, I've learned my ceiling on those is an over-30 men's slo-pitch league and karaoke.

One of the biggest hurdles and victories in any entrepreneur's business is knowing when and what to give up and what to delegate/ outsource to others. As a recent example, Alison and I created the UnPodcast, which would be our first foray into the world of podcasting and creating weekly content. As someone who blogs every few months when I feel like it, creating any kind of content schedule was daunting, to say the least. The podcast world is amazing and fickle; people want their episodes, and they want them when you say you're going to send them. Since the UnPodcast is really just Alison and I speaking casually but with microphones, I knew we'd have no lack of things to talk about. We had to decide if we were going to do everything ourselves, which would include recording, uploading, editing, and summarizing. We decided we would focus on our strengths, and not surprising to anyone who knows us, our strength is talking.

The biggest content bottleneck at UnMarketing is me. I don't like to work, and I don't like to do things when I'm told to do them. We were at a fork in the road: Do we bootstrap it like a classical podcast, or do the best possible and most likely to be created and shared weekly format? We chose the latter.

I invested in us and took Cliff Ravenscraft's podcast A to Z course and learned everything about the medium that I could. We then went out and found the best people to do the things we didn't want to do and removed our learning curve, because they were already the best at it. Who said you needed to be the best at everything? We hired Wayne Cochrane, from Wayne Cochrane Sound, who was the audio engineer on the first two audio books and Adam from Atomic Spark video to run a three-camera high-definition shoot of each episode in a studio we rent. We hired Rebecca Livermore to upload the weekly content to the UnPodcast.com site and to iTunes.

If we were going to be nine years late to the podcast party, we were gonna show up guns a-blazing!

Hiring others for their strengths can be challenging for entrepreneurs. We think we can do everything and often need to in the beginning. Most people I know who've started companies have done every task possible at one time or another. The thing is, when tasks you hate, or can't do as well as someone else, get in the way of the things you want or should be doing, you can't move forward in business.

For example, think about design and advertising agencies. Many of us start out doing our own marketing and design. We have to. But there comes a point in time when we need to hire experts and then let them do their jobs. Looking back, outsourcing tasks was a big part of taking the pulse of my company and making changes for the better. Here is one of my favorite examples of why outsourcing is so important to pulse.

I get the argument for putting advertising on vehicles; it's free space and doesn't cost you anything extra to have it flying around town once you cover the initial cost of the decal or wrap. Now before you start planning yours, that does not mean I think you should be wrapping your PT Cruiser in a giant version of your face,[2] logos, slogans, or yes,

---

[2] I'm looking at you, real estate guy who parks it at the front corner of the grocery store parking lot and leaves it there all day.

even QR codes, all of which cover our roads so much that we're almost immune to them, tuning them out like most advertising.

We just don't want to see any more ads on cars and trucks . . . unless of course, they are the ones from Shatto milk,[3] the independent dairy producer out of Kansas City who decided to put something a little different on its vehicles:

Amazing, right?

If you're going to put something on your vehicles, don't make it a reproduction of a newspaper ad. Nobody takes a picture of your mobile ad and shares it with their friends;[4] people share things that evoke emotions—and humor, done well, is the top one.

They even rock a store ad campaign for their new line of ice cream and its advertising:

---

[3] Best dairy name, ever. Especially if you're lactose intolerant.
[4] Otherwise known as that sought-after-thing called word of mouth.

The real key to this story is how the company came up with these campaigns in the first place.

I tweeted the Shatto milk account and asked how it came up with the idea, and the person replied, simply, that Shatto hadn't. The company hired an agency and then let the agency do its job. It was the agency staff who thought up the awesome trucks and ad campaign; Shatto simply hired them and trusted their concept. If you've ever been on the agency or consulting side of things, you just wept and possibly fainted after reading that. Imagine: A client hires you to be fun and creative and then gets out of the way to let you be fun and creative!

I don't know of any independent dairy producers in my city, or even in Canada, but I have heard of Shatto. Isn't that what marketing is supposed to do?

Taking the pulse of our businesses is how we take control over our growth and our success. It's the companies making the time to look inward that have the happiest and most productive creation. Think about the things you do every day and figure out what drives you.

Ask yourself two questions: What do I love to do? What do I need to do? And then look at ways to outsource the tasks that don't fit into those two categories. Then take a long look for what others can do better—we don't need to do everything in our companies. Designers, specialists, accountants, and others are all experts in their fields for a reason.

Last, one of the most challenging parts of taking the pulse of your company is valuing your own time. We can keep ourselves very busy and very broke by getting paid in coffees for brain-picking and giving away our expertise for free.

Not a week goes by where someone isn't asking to trade my expertise for a coffee. But helping one another out can't be a one-way street. If you don't value your own time, no one else will. There is always value in investing your time in a relationship, but just like those in our personal lives, business relationships can become toxic.

Part of writing a book is offering up a ton of knowledge at a small price. There isn't much I can say over a "quick coffee" that isn't included in here or in the other three books I've written. Then there is blogging, an expert's ideal forum to share information and experience and all at the low price of free.

Brain-picking, or access to the knowledge of others at a minimal cost, as one could call it, is one of the great things about building relationships online. I am much more likely to consider helping out someone whom I have connected to through social media than someone asking out of the blue. When you do connect with someone online whom you would like to ask for help, just remember to be appropriate. A follow is like accepting a request for a first date; you can't just show up and jump the gun. It's awkward . . . and it will certainly backfire.

24

Big Ass Chapter

BIG ASS FANS sells high-end, the only-one-you'll-ever-need-to-buy fans. The founder, Carey Smith, is as passionate about the quality of his product as he is about his suppliers, employees, and customers. The company not only pays well but respects and values all of those who come in contact with it.

What caught our attention was an article about how the company paid its employees 30 percent above the national median and 50 percent above Kentucky's median, where they are located. Then we read that during the economic downturn and recession, they didn't lay off a single employee.

"Smith's policy of paying employees well goes back to a remark he heard in his 20s when he worked for an insurance company. A senior executive said the insurer could afford to pay people much more than they did—but since employees were willing to accept low wages, why bother?"

The comment, and the attitude behind it, rankled Smith so much that he began thinking of starting an enterprise "where employees could share in the company's financial success."

And Big Ass Fans does just that. Smith pays out about 30 percent of the company's annual profits as bonuses. Although they dipped a bit during the recession, Smith takes pride in the fact that no employees were laid off.

"Not only is the no-layoffs policy good for company morale," Smith says, "it also saves Big Ass Fans thousands of dollars in recruiting and training new employees."[1]

So we read all that great stuff, and then we read the company's name.

That's what branding is really about.

I was lucky enough to speak to Carey, and I learned so much from him. It has been a highlight of research for *UnSelling,* and I encourage you to check out www.BigAssFans.com and see how business can be done. Since we really can't say enough good things about them, we decided to create a list of how we all can be a little better by being more like Big Ass Fans.

All You Need to Know about Business You Could Learn from Big Ass Fans

(with quotes from Carey Smith)

1. "The customer cannot be dissatisfied. That's how we get paid. Our response is always to help and recognize that the customer's problem is addressed. This can't happen unless employees and suppliers are treated with the same value." Big Ass Fans sets out to treat everyone well. From their suppliers and vendors, to their employees and customers, everyone is respected. It is not enough for a customer to buy a fan. Leaving a customer dissatisfied in any way is unacceptable, and it's everyone's responsibility to prevent that from happening.
2. "Relationship first—then making money is good business. If everyone is happy, then we will succeed—customers, supplier, and employees." Too many companies pad their sales numbers by cutting out suppliers and paying employees unfair wages, but not Big Ass Fans.

---

[1]Source: http://bit.ly/UnBigAss

3. Value and show respect to your customers, employees, and suppliers. "This is the only way I know how to work with people . . . people need to feel they are part of the problem and part of the solution."

4. Create great stuff and be passionate. We mentioned Big Ass Fans on the podcast, and Alison described the product as being ordinary, "just a fan." When we spoke on the phone, Carey was quick to let her know that they sold the very best fans, not "just fans." You could hear the passion and commitment to quality in his voice, and you can see it throughout the company.

5. Build a good environment that attracts good people. The company has a scholarship program for students out of high school to help them afford a college education. "When they finish school we hope they will come work with us, but if not then we have made a friend of someone who will be in a good position."

6. Value employee satisfaction. "If people are doing a job they don't like, it won't matter if you give them a raise." Big Ass Fans supports employees moving around to different positions within the company.

7. Set the tone. He doesn't like to be called boss. Carey says he is a "steward" and the company's product and ideas are something they all share.

8. Don't be a commodity. "If the only way you can think of to make more money is by cutting corners, then you are selling out—selling out over money." Commodities compete based only on cost, and you will end up losing.

9. Don't panic. Because Big Ass Fans didn't have any layoffs during the recession, when it ended, it had a full staff of trained, loyal employees. "Rehiring and training are expensive. How could I fire someone? I know their family. Am I just going to ruin that person's life to not lose money?"

10. Be a part of the community. "When you invest in the community, you know the pulse of those around you—your

(continued)

(continued)

customers and your employees." It becomes a lot easier to treat employees badly when you don't really know them—and a lot harder to get the most from them.

11. Last, if you follow numbers 1 through 10, you will make money. Making money isn't the primary goal; it's the result of hiring great people, creating innovative products, and developing a culture that treats everyone the way you would want to be treated. If the company doesn't succeed, then it can't keep doing all these great, innovative things. From 2009 to 2012, sales rose from $34 million to $87 million. In 2013, that number continued to go up to about $122 million. Guess this whole "treating people well" thing is good for business after all.

I learned a lot from Big Ass Fans. To me, that company really is the best example of what *UnSelling* is all about and how to put it into practice for your business. We spend a lot of time, especially in social media, learning from others what not to do. Well, Big Ass Fans is a lesson in what you should be doing to grow your business, improve your product and service, and treat others better. Let's make doing this kind of business the norm. That would definitely be a big ass improvement.

25

Direct versus Moral Offense

SOMEWHERE ALONG THE way, I became the go-to for customer advocacy online. People are always sending me examples of bad service and poor customer experiences—and I love it.[1] Social media has created an even playing field for customers by providing endless information and a channel to voice and share their experiences and knowledge. "The customer knows best" isn't just an expression anymore—they really do.

The list of offenses by companies varies from long waiting times, faulty products, and understaffed service departments to high crimes of discrimination and cruelty. How we as customers decide to field this treatment is key to the concept of *UnSelling*—these experiences matter—they shape our buying patterns and the offenders' branding and success.

Along the way and over the years, hearing all these stories has become one of the best things about running UnMarketing and social media for me.

I have divided the types of offenses into two categories, which help explain why we react in certain ways to each type. They are direct

---

[1] If you have a story to share, you can e-mail me scott@un-marketing.com.

offenses and moral offenses. Let's take a look and see what each one means.

A direct offense happens to you . . . or to me . . . or to both of us if we're out for coffee with the same rude waiter. These offenses are our personal stories of contacts with brands that go wrong. Whatever the pulse point may be, it happened to us. Direct offenses can challenge our morals or be about quality and/or service.

Moral offenses can happen to you or to other people. These are the offenses that challenge our morals about the world around us. When a brand makes a racist statement, that is a moral offense. Not everyone may be offended—some may even come to the brand's defense—but for many, these offenses are as damaging to the pulse, if not more so, than any direct offense. Standing up for one another is one of the best things about the strength of an online community, and moral outrage will start fast and build quickly.

As we've seen in looking at customer pulse, our experiences are shaped by brand interactions—for better or for worse. In the next few sections we're going to look at some examples of direct and moral offenses and consider how these have shaped customer pulse. In a world where a single story of one customer sitting at one takeout counter can spread to a million people overnight, brands can no longer ignore the power of consumer advocacy—and I love it.

26

Offensive Real Estate

AN AWESOME FRIEND, who wishes to remain nameless, received this very UnAwesome letter after the death of a neighbor, on Valentine's Day of all days. It came to her door, and she had to share it with us—because it has to be the most insensitive real estate pitch we've ever seen. And that's saying something.

Dear friend,

The Real Estate Agency of UnAwesome [name changed to protect the UnInnocent] would like to extend our condolences for the loss of your neighbour. We were all devastated by his passing. Your building has lost a powerhouse on a lot of levels. As owners of the agency, we have big shoes to fill professionally.

He was our coworker, and a dear friend to a number of people in our office. We want to continue his legacy of quality real estate services for his clients. Please know that we will give you the same attention to detail and rapid response that he himself would have.

(continued)

(*continued*)

To that end, please call or e-mail my partner or myself [they included their business cards in the letter] to schedule a convenient time to have a short conversation with you so we can learn about your real estate needs. We will pair you with the best agent for your situation, goals and personality. Our clients' satisfaction is our number one priority and we feel a special responsibility to give the utmost service to his clients.

Signed, with e-mails and phone numbers.

Gives you a warm fuzzy feeling, doesn't it?

Our friend was horrified and decided then and there never, ever to use their services. The offense came right to her door, trying to leverage the loss of a neighbor. Who would read something like this and call them? They want to pair the community with agents who match their personality! Well, I'm thinking they would have to scrape the bottom of the barrel of humans to do that.

Direct offenses happen to us. We see them, or in this case read them, firsthand. I can picture our friend standing in her house realizing just what this agency was trying to do and thinking, "Wait until Scott sees this!"

I shared the story on the UnPodcast and here with you, taking a direct offense and spreading the word. The story is certainly offensive enough to qualify as a moral offense. I can't say this enough to businesses: The time for your sales pitch is *not* during a tragedy! You should not leverage disasters and loss for personal gain. All that happens is that you come off looking like the callus, self-centered person you are. This is the time to help or be quiet—and I do not mean help as in services your company sells. Offer condolences and then get out of the way.

27

The Moral Offense

BUSINESSES ARE ALL made up of people. That's a strength when it comes to social and branding, but it can also be the most challenging part.

People. There's just no accounting for them.

We believe things and share our ideas. We have hate and preconceptions. Public relations departments were created to craft messages for just that reason. We couldn't just let the owners and employees speak; that would be dangerous . . .

Well, in the today's world of social media and connectivity, we all have a voice. And some of these voices offend other people's voices. A moral offense is one of these. Even if the treatment didn't happen to you personally, just hearing about it can be enough to change your mind about purchases.

When news spread that the new CEO Brendan Eich of Mozilla had made a donation to support Prop 8, a proposition in California to change law and make gay marriage illegal. It was ruled to be unconstitutional, but supporters of the bill who had made donations greater than $1,000 were made public domain, and the CEO's name was on the list.

Opponents of Eich and his discriminatory stance took to the Internet to demand his resignation. The online dating site OkCupid, went as far as to put this message on its home page:

> Hello there, Mozilla Firefox user. Pardon this interruption of your OkCupid experience.
>
> Mozilla's new CEO, Brendan Eich, is an opponent of equal rights for gay couples. We would therefore prefer that our users not use Mozilla software to access OkCupid.
>
> Politics is normally not the business of a website, and we all know there's a lot more wrong with the world than misguided CEOs. So you might wonder why we're asserting ourselves today. This is why: we've devoted the last ten years to bringing people—all people—together. If individuals like Mr. Eich had their way, then roughly 8% of the relationships we've worked so hard to bring about would be illegal. Equality for gay relationships is personally important to many of us here at OkCupid. But it's professionally important to the entire company. OkCupid is for creating love. Those who seek to deny love and instead enforce misery, shame, and frustration are our enemies, and we wish them nothing but failure.

The backlash led to Eich's resignation.

This is a great example of how companies and consumers react to moral offenses. To be outraged, we didn't need to know Eich personally, or even be a Mozilla customer. The issue runs deeper, to the point where those entirely removed from the situation can still be so angry that they will demand a change out of principle.

On the other side is the moral sale, where we make purchase choices because of the moral stand of a company or individual. There are people who would have become Mozilla customers simply because of Eich's stance on gay marriage. They'd make this choice even if the product or service didn't meet their needs in other ways—only on moral grounds.

Environmentalists will go out of their way to buy groceries at stores without plastic bags. People who believe Walmart is evil will choose local businesses every time, even if prices and convenience fall by the wayside.

As we touched on in the last chapter, leveraging news events is one of the surest ways to offend morally. There is an entire school of marketing based on newsjacking—choosing to leverage events. The worst example of newsjacking I've seen happened on Martin Luther King, Jr., Day. On this historic day, 50 years ago, one of the greatest speeches in history was given. "I Have a Dream" by Dr. Martin Luther King, Jr. It gave me chills when I heard it for the first time when I was eight, and it still does today.

So why not celebrate this historic day by making it about golf?

Shame on the Golf Channel. I cannot fathom someone sitting around a desk saying, "I know how we can go viral! Let's newsjack! Tweet it up!"

Stop. Doing. This.

Stop trying to piggyback off holidays and celebrations by making it about you.

Stop trying to go viral or to trend.

You know what a brand should do today? Nothing. Or show some respect and send out a tweet like, "On this historic day 50 years ago, Martin Luther King, Jr., had a dream. Thank you for changing the world." Or whatever it is you want to say.

You don't need to leverage this speech. You don't need to leverage natural disasters. You don't need to capitalize on civil unrest.

You need to be human. It's not always about business.

28

The Politics of Engagement

THE TWO WORDS *government* and *community* are an interesting pair. Government is meant to serve the community, yet it often seems they have trouble wrapping their heads around our needs. In social media, this lack of congruence is amplified—with very public results.

For example, in the community, news happens quickly. We share what's happening around us on social media, where there is an expectation of getting a quick response. However, a recent article in the Globe and Mail[1] reported:

> Newly disclosed documents from Industry Canada show how teams of bureaucrats often work for weeks to sanitize each lowly tweet, in a medium that's supposed to thrive on spontaneity and informality.

Tweets are being put in front of the eyes and minds of staff and put through a 12-step process of editing and rewriting before they are shared. This has got to be the opposite of the spirit of Twitter, where conversations are quick and tweets are rarely seen past a few moments.

---

[1] Source: http://bit.ly/TweetsTakeWeeks

The new information also showed that different departments had arrangements in place a few weeks before tweets were shared by Industry Canada to retweet them, because they knew retweets were valuable. A retweet has value only if it's based in the quality of the content, not because it is prearranged.

The article went on to say,

> Public servants vet draft tweets for hashtags, syntax, policy compliance, retweeting, French translation and other factors. Policy generally precludes tweeting on weekends, and the minister's personal Twitter handle must be kept out of departmental tweets, though his name and title are often included.

Keeping office hours can be very problematic online. Setting expectations for replies is great, but what happens when a disaster or other community issue happens, Twitter rallies, and our government can't reply because it's Saturday? A two-week lead time certainly can't prepare tweets in response to a need on a weekday, let alone a weekend.

Taking the tools and ways of doing things that work in newspaper or press releases and thinking you can simply make them 140 characters and post to Twitter will not work. If you want to kill spontaneity and honest conversation, just throw in bureaucracy. If you truly are "for the people" and one of their community, you can and should be where the community is.

The following are a few Canadian mayors who make my country proud. I'm using Canadian examples because not only are we awesome and modest, but since Mayor Rob Ford changed the world's view of Toronto,[2] we need all the positive stories we can get.

Hands down, one of my favorite people on Twitter, Mayor Nenshi of Calgary Alberta, has the perfect personality to be a politician on Twitter. Funny, personable with a half-cup of snarkiness, his tweets not only are read by constituents but shared all over the world. I've tried to organize a trade between him and Toronto's mayor, but so far, no dice.

In *The Book of Business Awesome/UnAwesome*, we highlighted his ability to handle people throwing jabs at him:

---

[2]Feel free to crack some jokes here.

He also knows how to make people feel like they're superstars:

When we look at these examples from the awesome @Nenshi, we tend to think it's the platform that makes the connections happen—and that's a huge problem. Twitter is just a tool. Mayor Nenshi is a great mayor, who communicates well with his city, and sometimes that happens on Twitter. Twitter doesn't make people like, or dislike, a politician. The site is neutral. Just like a paintbrush won't make me a successful painter, social media can't take a jerk and turn them into an adored politician. It's just a tool, one that amplifies and shares whatever we already are.

As we see here from Pat Garofalo, a Minnesota House Representative:

 Rep. Pat Garofalo
@PatGarofalo

Let's be honest, 70% of teams in NBA could fold tomorrow + nobody would notice a difference w/ possible exception of increase in streetcrime

7:33 PM - 9 Mar 2014

1,944 RETWEETS 588 FAVORITES

They say that authenticity is king on social media, unless, of course, you are authentically a jackass. I especially enjoy how he started his racist tweet with "let's be honest." That really sets a nice tone to the whole thing.

Authenticity can come through in ways other than original tweets; we also see it in replies and what politicians choose to share with their followers, as we see from Mayor Watson from Ottawa, Ontario:

Jim Watson
@JimWatsonOttawa

The Pride Flag will fly at Ottawa City Hall until the end of the Olympics. #Sochi2014

1:13 PM - 6 Feb 2014

2,601 RETWEETS 2,180 FAVORITES

Source: Reproduced by permission of Jim Watson.

Some people took exception to his tweet, amazingly enough, and he reacted perfectly:

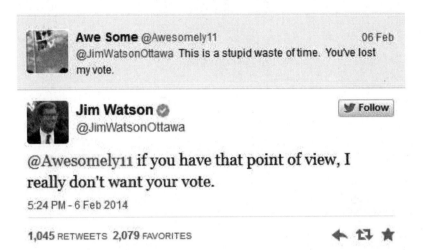

Like me, before seeing this tweet, many of you had never heard of Jim Watson. I immediately became a big fan of his. Politicians are meant to take positions, make them known, and allow the public opinion to decide where they stand. We are meant to want people in office who represent our opinions. It's one of the things I love about them airing opinions on Twitter, because for good or for bad, it's better to know how they feel. Then we can decide if they should or should not represent us.

This also raises the question, does this exchange make a difference when a lot of the eyes seeing it will not be voting in Watson's city? Does the sentiment about him matter? I believe it does. It can affect people's decisions about where to move or visit and can influence where businesses consider setting up shop. As cities we work hard to attract tourism and new investments and keep our good ones here. And having community leaders is a big part of that—or, unfortunately, vice versa. Just ask anyone who's changed his or her mind lately about holding an event in Toronto. Anyone want a mayor? Ugh.

29

Insubordinate Customers

As CUSTOMERS, WE experience moral and direct offenses by companies all the time. But how about the other way around? Every business owner I know has at least one story of a customer gone wrong—someone they just could not please and at some point needed to cut loose.

We could look at insubordinate customers as trolls, but we shouldn't. Trolls are all about hate, and they wield it blindly in all directions. Trolls jump onto our business Facebook page, leave a comment about someone's mom, and run away. We know not to give trolls our time or energy, no matter how tempting that might be. We know not to feed the trolls.

An insubordinate customer is more work than a troll, less obvious from the start, and can be worth our time. In some businesses and some positions, every customer seems insubordinate. This job would be soooo much easier if it wasn't for those pesky customers! Right?

We become immediately defensive and try to pass issues and blame along to someone else as quickly as possible. This is where we have two options as companies: An issue brought to us by a customer can either be our problem to solve or not our problem and something to dismiss. In the best work environments, the customer is always worth problem solving for.

Most of the time an insubordinate customer is just frustrated and unwilling to follow the chain of command we've crafted for complaints. Like the strong-willed child of our business lives, the things that work on all our other customers just won't seem to work on them. We try to control customers much the same way we do employees: insisting they follow protocol and procedure. When they won't, we struggle and become frustrated ourselves. From there, issues have a way of snowballing into ALL-CAPS wonderlands.

Insubordinate customers are often down to their last straw with a brand. Who isn't angry by the time they're bounced around to three different departments in a company for resolution? We don't start out insubordinate, but we get there, one small thing at a time. When we look at pulse from the viewpoint of the company, we may not always recognize a particular issue as a brand's last-straw interaction because the individual issue seems small. We don't necessarily see the past pulse points that have led up to this single straw breaking the customer's back. That's why each issue, no matter how small, needs to be treated with respect and care. Unfortunately, it's usually once the issues snowball that customers start getting the attention they deserve.

Social media is blamed for a lot of these snowballs, but it shouldn't be. Social is just another communication tool, one that can only highlight an issue you were already having and amplify it. Now, of course, we'd all rather manage an insubordinate customer in the privacy of a two-way phone call, rather than the public forum of our company blog, but that just makes the opportunity to resolve the issue bigger and shareable. If your customer service staff dismiss customers and are unhelpful, that isn't a social media problem; that is a hiring problem. How our customer chooses to come to us with an issue is really outside of our business to control. We need to focus instead on training and empowering employees to solve issues with knowledge and respect.

So what happens in those situations where you try everything and still can't please a customer, or genuinely feel you're being taken advantage of? We spoke about one of these situations on the UnPodcast, when we looked at the case of the used razor blades.

A high-end custom razor blade company had reached out to me about an issue it was having in social media. A customer had returned a package he'd claimed to have ordered from them for a refund, because he said the shipment had arrived used, with hair on the blades.

Before returning the shipment, he'd gone ahead and posted pictures of the blades publicly on the company's Facebook page.

The company checked the serial number on the product in his picture and found it did not match any of their products. The man was lying and maliciously spreading false, and downright yucky, information about this company.

So, what do you do?

Sometimes in business you have to manage the crazy; there's just no other way around it. When someone like this attacks your credibility, you want to lash out. I advised the company to pick its public battles and not engage with the individual. Management needed to choose whether this was worth their time and energy. Was this one to go to war with, or should they be taking the high road? In the end, they decided to send the customer a shipment of replacement blades similar to those he was looking for and flagging the customer so he could never get away with this kind of thing again.

Always remember, you can spend so much time in business fighting fires that you forget to set things in place to keep them from happening in the first place. Having a system for flagging insubordinate customers and keeping track of interactions between sales, customer service, and your market is very important. That way, when you get the angry customer on his or her fourth call in, you're ready.

There is a story about two people who walk up to a river and see people drowning. One runs into the water and starts dragging people out one by one. Even once he's exhausted, he keeps running back in and saving people. The other stands there for a few minutes and runs away, leaving his friend to keep going in and out, over and over again.

When the man sees his friend running away, he shouts after him, "Can't you see all these people? Where are you going?!"

"I'm going upstream to stop whoever is throwing all these people in the river."

When you find yourself dealing with angry customers until you're exhausted, don't forget to figure out what's getting them angry in the first place. We need to be taking these situations and using them to fix broken, outdated policies and faulty products and services. That way we can stop the insubordination before it happens.

30

Outrage Outreach

REACTION, REBELLION, AND rage do not take the weekends off. Whether brands decide to be part of the social media conversation or not, they need to be listening. I am a huge opponent of automation in social, except when it comes to listening. There are companies that can help you, such as Meshfire[1] and Trackur, or it can be as simple as setting up a Google search for your brand and any keywords for your industry you want to keep an eye on. As we spoke about in the Delta story, even search for common misspellings of your name by irate tweeters so blind with anger that they can't type and fume at the same time.

How a business manages angry customers matters. In *The Book of Business Awesome/UnAwesome*, we spent a lot of time talking about how to handle outrage. When it hits the fan, it's not time to hide behind the fan; it's time to be awesome. A properly handled online outrage can leave the company looking better after the screwup than before. It's all about company reaction: authenticity, immediacy, and appropriate response.

A perfect example of how to handle outrage successfully was from Liberty Bottleworks, a water bottle company from Washington State.

---

[1] I'm on their board of advisors so that makes them awesome!

Cofounder Ryan Clark's reply to an angry customer led to a ton of exposure and positive reviews for his company. A customer, furious that the
company had not been fast enough in fixing an issue with her order,
posted the following all-caps wonder on the company's Facebook page.

> DON'T DO BUSINESS WITH THIS COMPANY IF YOU
> WANT IT HANDLED RIGHT. THEY WAIT OVER A WEEK
> TO LET YOU KNOW—THEY LOST YOUR PAYMENT—
> THEY PROVIDE A PHONE NUMBER THAT NO ONE
> EVER ANSWERS. IF YOU HAVE A DEADLINE—LIKE
> CHRISTMAS—FORGET ABOUT IT. product is great—
> COMPANY is NOT.

So what do you do in this situation? The anger is out there, for all to
see. You've worked long and hard to get your company off the ground,
and here is someone trying to bring it down. If we are always trying to
move people into being ecstatic customers, we sure have a long way to
go with this one. At least she says she likes the product . . . although
that is the only thing not in all caps.

Here is how Ryan Clark, chief operating officer (COO) of Liberty
Bottleworks, decided to reply:

> Ryan Clark, Liberty's Co-founder and COO, here. I normally do
> not hop into Facebook rants but this one needed addressed. First
> of all, Ms. X thank you for your oder [sic] and your desire to sup-
> port American Companies, Job Creation, Green Manufacturing
> and the Hiring of Vets. We did receive your numerous voicemails
> and emails. The bucks stops with me. This will I am sure will [sic]
> upset you but . . . my customer service team will not be helping
> you on the weekends. Your voicemail stated "it is the holidays,
> you should be working" and you [sic] email stated, "instead of
> doing my Christmas cards and enjoying the holiday spirit, I was
> dealing with this". Perhaps, you need to spend a bit more time
> embracing the holiday spirit. You see, my employees were home

with their families doing their cards, baking cookies, etc. Family first, product second. If you want immediate service on a Saturday, try supporting your local retail establishment such as, Bill and Pauls Sporthaus, People's Food Coop, Barnes Ace Hardware. As to your original complaint, we emailed within 24 hours of your order concerning the Paypal issue. Second, we called you first thing this morning in response to your angry voicemails but you hung up on us when we introduced ourselves saying, "I never want to speak with anyone from your company." Ms. X, we pride ourselves on doing things well, we pride ourselves on doing things right, we pride ourselves on doing things the American way. Not instant gratification, 24 hour shopping on Thanksgiving type of American way but, family and country type of American way. The way our grandparents did things type of American way. I am sorry you are upset and I will gladly give you your money back, but I am not sorry our employees were enjoying the holidays. That right is not exclusive to you. If you would like to discuss this is [sic] on the phone you may call my personal cell (509) XXX-XXXX. If I do not get back with you right away understand I may be eating dinner with my wife and kids. Please be advised we will not be shipping you your order, you will not be charged. I will not do business with anyone that threatens my employees the way you have. Merry Christmas!

There is a lot of awesome in this reply. First, he replied. He actually was listening—saw the post—and decided that the woman deserved to be responded to. Most companies never make it this far, and the anger just sits there on the brand Facebook page. It just sits there for everyone to see, looking very much ignored and unimportant.

So he showed up; 2 points for Liberty Bottleworks!

He addressed the customer's concerns in an educated manner, showing that he had looked into her post and took the concerns seriously. He defended his staff. Time and time again, we see that the way a company treats its staff is reflected in the way it treats its market. And perhaps most important—and why I think the reply spread so far online—he took a stand for his company.

Leaders need to take stands, and that's what a company needs in the face of social media outrage: a leader or leaders who aren't afraid to stand in the way and take the heat.

He could have left the customer without a reply. He could have let someone else with less of a founder kind of role manage her. He could have thrown his staff under the bus. But he did none of these things. He stood by a value held by the company, and the results were awesome. The company received a huge amount of positive attention and sales as a result.

How can you look at this story and think connecting online with customers, even the angry ones, doesn't matter?

31

The Impenetrable Brand

THERE ARE CUSTOMER-COMPANY relationships that are tough to crack. Loyalty can be strong, and even when direct and moral offenses occur, many customers hang on tight. These companies seem to have achieved a status where they can do no wrong. This leaves us to wonder how far they would need to push us to lose business. We call these the impenetrable brands.

We could also call this chapter "Why Scott Says Alison Can't Have Nice Things."

For example, Lululemon.

Some of you may not know this about me, but I actually don't do yoga. I know you're shocked, but I don't. I do have a pair of Lululemon shorts that the company sent to me a few years ago, and they are amazing, nonchaffing, and comfy.

Alison loves yoga *and* actually does it. So when we were recording a podcast and I let her know about Chip Wilson, former CEO of Lululemon and some of the horrible things he's said, she was pretty shocked. Here are my two faves:

> Frankly some women's bodies just actually don't work for
> (wearing Lululemon pants) . . . it's really about the rubbing

through the thighs, how much pressure there is over a period of time and, how much they use it. (*Reply to a Bloomberg TV report about consumer complaints*)

The reasons the Japanese liked my former skateboard brand, "Homeless," was because it had an L in it and a Japanese marketing firm wouldn't come up with a brand name with an L in it. L is not in their vocabulary. It's a tough pronunciation for them. So I thought, next time I have a company, I'll make a name with three Ls in it and see if I can get three times the money. It's kind of exotic for them. I was playing with Ls and came up with Lululemon. It's funny to watch them try to say it. (*2004 interview with* National Post Business *magazine*)

So, of course, seeing these as two statements entirely out of line with Alison's sensibilities, I assumed she would be shocked and immediately burn her yoga pants.

Alison: But they are my favorites.

Scott: So even though the guy is basically saying it's fat women's fault about the product issues and that they shouldn't be wearing the pants anyway . . . and even though he's being completely discriminatory and offensive with the L comment . . . you still are going to buy their pants!?

Alison: But they are my favorites . . .

Scott: Okay, so exactly what would Lululemon need to do to lose your business? Assuming the pants stayed the same.

Alison: Well, if they were outfitting soldiers in a world war or something, I probably would buy other pants.

Scott: They would need to be the official clothing sponsor of an evil empire for you to stop.

Alison: Ya, well, at least to probably stop . . .

To Alison, Lululemon is an impenetrable brand. She's tried others, and these are her favorites. She doesn't care about the cost, even though it certainly can be prohibitive. The quality of the product is all she cares about when making a yoga pant purchase, so evil empire notwithstanding, she's picking Lululemon every time.

I give you example number two: Martha Stewart.

Alison loves Martha Stewart. Anytime something is especially delicious, it seems to be a Martha Stewart recipe. And although we have already figured out that I don't do yoga, I do like to eat. So when I asked Alison on the UnPodcast if she was upset when Martha Stewart publicly slammed bloggers, I shouldn't have been too surprised by the response.

Scott: And then Martha said, "Who are those bloggers? They're not trained editors at *Vogue* magazine. Writing recipes that aren't tested, that aren't necessarily very good. Or are copies of everything that really good editors have created and done. Bloggers create a popularity, but they are not the experts."

Alison: I didn't know Martha was a trained editor at *Vogue!*

Scott: I think you may be missing the point here. Did you hear what she said!? She's totally slamming bloggers! Says they aren't experts!

Alison: Ya, that sounds like something she would say. I'm sure food bloggers take some of her traffic.

Scott: That's it!? You aren't even a tiny bit offended.

Alison: Well, I'm no Martha Stewart. At least she isn't going to jail again. I don't really care if she thinks bloggers are experts or not; that's really up to their audience.

Scott: So she is insulting the hard work of tons of people, some of whom you know personally, and you don't care? Are you still going to visit her site and buy her books and stuff?

Alison: OF COURSE I am. I don't care what she says about anything other than recipes. Every compliment I have ever received for cooking or baking is because of that woman. She's my roast turkey Jesus.

Like Lululemon before her, Roast Turkey Jesus can do no wrong because her product is considered outstanding by the customer. I don't need to ask Alison to know that even if the evil empire clothed by Lululemon went to dinner every night in Martha's kitchen that Alison would still use Martha's chicken pot pie recipe—because sometimes products are so good, they become impenetrable brands.

Namaste, Martha.

32

Pivot

WHEN WE LOOKED at pulse, we saw how each interaction between a brand and customer could move the pulse line up or down. There was never a neutral brand experience, and these experiences ranged from direct contact with a frontline salesperson to social media direct and indirect interactions. Most of the time, these pulse points create small changes up or down, and they cumulatively create an overall experience that puts individuals in varying degrees of happy places with your brand, ranging from a flatline to open-to-competition, and from a current customer to an ecstatic one.

Every once in a while, however, we see a big change in the pulse, where the contact is so extraordinary that the line changes directions dramatically. We call this a *pivot point*.

Pivot points happen in stories like the Amelia Island Ritz-Carlton and the Hurn family, where an experience is so great that the brand pulse skyrockets, taking along with it impressions like mine and yours. Negative pivot points occur when the experience is a moral or direct offense that discounts any of our other needs for convenience and cost—to the point where we simply refuse to be a customer because we don't want to be associated with the brand values. A pivot point can be as simple as trying out a product, loving it, and becoming a loyal customer—or hating it and never taking a chance on the brand again.

Pivot can also happen inside a business related to the industry it operates in. We saw this time and time again when conducting interviews for *UnSelling*: Successful companies were not afraid to make big changes when presented with industry and technology shifts. You will see a perfect example of this in a few chapters when we talk about AutoTrader's decision to close down the print division of its business.

Business history is filled with successful brands that pivot and those that didn't. Pivot deniers are left behind with "what has always worked," unwilling or unable to move forward with their industry. Hindsight is always 20/20, of course, but as business owners, we need to be learning from these stories and focusing on the pulse of our companies and industries so that we see changes coming and are ready for them. As employees, we are often the most in touch with these changes and need to be empowered to share our experiences with our coworkers and managers so that we can continue to improve and stay relevant.

At UnMarketing, I work in an industry that is changing daily. Social media and technology are young, and the rules are still being made as we go along. New game-changing sites pop up constantly, and the pull for my and your attention is never ending. I spend most of my time keeping on top of the industry so that I can share that expertise with you and audiences around the world. Because when changes happen, we need to be ready to pivot.

33

Hiring at Rock Bottom

IF YOU DON'T fly a lot, or tweet a lot, or work on the go a lot, then you may not understand the anxious feeling when a flight attendant tells you it's now time to put away your phone for takeoff. Did you in fact remember to answer that important e-mail? What if the customer replies in flight, and you aren't around for a quick enough response? What if someone tweets about coffee, and you aren't there to reply? How will the social world ever go on without you for 4 hours and 20 minutes in the air?

I know, I know . . . none of us are really that important. And if our companies are so big and busy that a few hours in air will really cause a problem, it may be time to do some hiring. Just saying.

I did once have someone tweet to me from Europe that he loved my book, and because I was asleep and failed to reply within his dictated 5-hour window, he had turned and called me a fraud on Twitter—all before I'd opened my eyes.

So I get it. When you live on your phone, sometimes putting it away can be hard.

Now, for most of us, that is the worst thing that will happen. Someone won't be replied to quickly enough, and mild irritation may result. Not really a big deal, right?

Well, add in a severe case of racism and a position as a public relations expert, and a whole lot can happen during an international flight.

Justine Sacco sent the tweet heard around the world in 2013, just as she boarded a flight to Africa. Her tweet was as offensive as they come, especially considering her position as communications director. She wrote, "Going to Africa. Hope I don't get AIDS. Just kidding. I'm white!"[1]

The outrage that followed happened while Sacco was without Internet, because, of course, she was in the air headed to Africa. She landed to online outrage and to find she had been fired from her job.

Although she issued an apology, she may forever be known for the racist tweet and subsequent job loss.

At the time of the tweet, there were a lot of different opinions about what happened—from total outrage, to a cry for forgiveness. I do not feel badly for her, or for the unfortunate growing number like her, who share their hate and prejudice online and feel the backlash.

There were even some who said they would gladly hire her after this, because she was so unlikely to be a repeat offender considering how harshly the world had reacted. I cannot say strongly enough how wrong I think this is. You know who you should hire if you don't want an employee who tweets racist statements? Someone who isn't a racist! Ta-da!

To think that a good, qualified person would be less desirable than one who had supposedly hit rock bottom online makes me furious. The Internet has a way of showing people's true colors. Behind the shield of a keyboard and screen, we can be so much more our real, mean selves sometimes. We should not be hiring at the bottom of the barrel, hoping an extreme reaction is sending someone pivoting in a new direction. Our employees are our brand and in the best position for positive, UnSelling interactions with customers. We need to be hiring accordingly.

We focus a lot of attention on the effects online mistakes like this one can have on a brand. Back in Chapter 17, I shared my Delta story with you and we saw how one employee's bad behavior (a rude flight attendant) changed my experience with an entire company—and

---

[1]Source: http://bit.ly/HorribleTweet

then another employee's amazing engagement on Twitter set it right. It is important to remember that the effects of a negative brand-customer interaction can do more than affect the brand—it can affect the individual and their future. Your online history is never more than a Google search away. If you've been wrapped up in some online racism or other bad Sacco-like behavior, remember it can follow you into future interviews, prospective employer searches, and even into your personal relationships.

34

From the Walkman to the iPod

OFTEN, COMPANIES MAKE pivot-type changes in response to changes in their industry. The most successful pivots seem almost ahead of the times, changing according to things seen coming, sensing where people's needs are moving, setting trends, and making leaps. What sets these companies apart? Is it access to more information, or maybe their willingness to take the information around them into account, rather than sticking with what has always worked? Maybe it's vision, access to research tools, or a certain unique experience or story by a founder who just believed the idea was going to work.

In the next few chapters, we're going to look at some industries that have changed and why some companies have been able to navigate these changes successfully while others were left behind. The companies unable or unwilling to make these changes find themselves outdated and unnecessary, to the same market that once kept them busy.

Most competition can be avoided by keeping your customers happy. But what about when no matter how great your product or service has been, the market simply shifts away from needing you? Because even if your Walkman was in perfect shape out of the box, you would still be buying an iPod. That's industry shift guiding product success.

When we looked at pulse earlier, we saw how external factors are always pushing on the pulse line to affect experience. When these are fairly small or constant, they lead to equally small or constant changes in the pulse. When large shifts happen in industries, their effects are equally felt. So when an entire industry changes, we see companies changing more dramatically to keep up.

When you travel a lot, or live in a major city, you learn a lot about taxis: the ins and outs, where to find them, how much to pay. In Las Vegas, they won't pick you up on the strip unless you are at a hotel in their line. In Istanbul, if you don't speak the language, bring along a card from your hotel so you know how to get back. In Thailand, license faces and driver faces may not always match, so maybe rent a scooter instead. In New York, just do whatever the locals are doing. And take the taxi to Shake Shack . . .

I have taken a lot of taxis. So when we were in New Orleans and heading out for dinner, I wasn't shy about walking out of the hotel and looking for one. I let the bellhop know we'd be needing one that accepted credit cards and was pretty shocked that none of the cars outside waiting could. I was even more surprised when a bike rickshaw pulled up and told me she'd be happy to take us and that she accepted cards no problem.

We checked the fare, which seemed great, and hopped up. It was a cool way to see the city, and she gave us some recommendations, one of which we ended up trying for dinner the next night. We got to our stop, she pulled out her iPhone with the Square app,[1] and she easily took our fare and e-mailed me a receipt. So very simple.

The ways in which we pay for things is one industry that has changed tremendously over the past few years. Here we were, in a major city, and the taxis wouldn't take credit cards (and therefore our business), but a person on a bike could—all from her phone. Needing to pay for things hasn't changed, but the delivery methods have.

Like giving money to a New Orleans bike taxi, here are some other industries that have changed:

1. *Publishing (textbooks, magazines, books)*: Content delivery is no longer about paper, and there are no used copies in the digital world.

---

[1] https://squareup.com/sell-in-store

2. *Encyclopedias*: As a child I would spend hours reading the encyclo-pedia. Today we have Wikipedia—and endless ways to learn and seem like we know what we're talking about. I never need to forget a song lyric or a movie line.

3. *Telephones*: Forty percent of all Americans now don't have a land-line. The mobile phone is prolific.

4. *Travel*: From bookings, to reviews, to accessing language translators and maps, the world is now right at our fingertips to explore. Sites such as Airbnb are changing where we stay; Yelp, where we eat; and Kayak, where we book.

5. *Real estate*: House listings are no longer a realtor's asset. With sites such as Trulia, what else do you bring to the table?

6. *Charity and fund-raising*: Indiegogo allows us to crowdfund ideas, SMS allows us to text donations, and we find new causes to support every day through social media.

7. *Capital raising*: All it takes is a Kickstarter with a good idea and decent size audience to get a company going.

8. *Music and radio*: Napster started change for most industries. From iTunes to Pandora, we're listening more than ever before, but dif-ferently.

9. *Movies*: Does anyone remember when Netflix only sent DVDs? We just canceled our cable.

10. *Time delivery*: I remember the day we needed a watch to tell time, or that's all a watch did.

11. *Payment processing*: As seen, you now can fit a Square peg through a round hole and be a merchant.

12. *Education*: More and more universities are offering their curricu-lums online for free.

Some of the industries we will look at are music, publishing, fund-raising, investment capital raising, automotive, and even some cellular providers for extra fun. With hindsight on our side, we can learn from others' choices, apply them to our own industries, and see what made the difference.

35

Why I Didn't Invent Spanx

THE MIND OF an entrepreneur is a funny thing. We share as many similarities as we do differences, but basically it all comes down to us all being unemployable, doesn't it? The more we study brands and the things that shape and create successful ones, the more it comes back to people. The people on the front lines, the salespeople, those driving research and development, those working human resources and customer service—great businesses have great people. Often, the most prolific brands have someone else, someone just as important: the founder.

When we spoke to Big Ass Fans' Carey Smith about his role, he told us how he preferred to be considered a steward versus a boss. His way of treating others sets the tone for the company, and it shows in every step along the way.

Does a great company need a founder in its story to make it successful? No. Does a great story make people want to hear more about a brand? Absolutely. I started UnMarketing because I was tired of seeing people market the way they hated to be marketed to themselves. I couldn't suggest clients use the same marketing ways I did everything I could to avoid, including cold calling and skeezy social media spamming. And I knew we could do better, and people would love it.

When I decided I hated the buy or good-bye of traditional marketing, I started UnMarketing.

In the life of an entrepreneur, more than a week rarely goes by that we don't see some other company we wish we'd also started. Remember those Silly Band things? Seriously, why didn't I think of an elastic band in a shape that my kids would need 100 packs of!? I totally had a book about an orphan wizard on my brain for years! And do not even get me started on those stands that hold your iPad in the bathroom. Pure genius. When I wanted to take my iPad into the bathroom, all I did was bring an extra chair in there with me . . .

- When I found a movie 9 weeks after it was due back to Blockbuster, all I did was pretend I'd never rented it.
- Reed Hastings started Netflix.
- When I got frustrated by the busy tone I got when trying to reach someone I was dating, all I did was try to call back later using my rotary dial phone.
- Sandra Lerner and her then-husband Len Bosack designed the multiprotocol router and founded Cisco.
- When I had acne in high school, all I did was hope it wasn't picture day.
- Katie Rodan and Kathy Fields took their experience and dermatology degrees and founded Proactiv.
- If I ever had enough money to buy a plane for fun and then it broke, all I might do is stay home and roll around naked in the money.
- William E. Boeing decided he could do better, built a seaplane with a friend, and started Boeing.
- When I used to get frustrated in college about forgetting my USB, all I did was "borrow" one from someone else.
- Drew Houston decided there should be a better way and developed Dropbox.
- Apple, HP, Amazon, Harley-Davidson, and Google, among others, all claim the garage as their founding home.
- When my son got frustrated that he couldn't get a custom wrestling toy with exactly the outfit of his choosing, all I did was write a stern

tweet to the manufacturer and reminisce about the times of Andre the Giant and Superfly Snuka.

- Maxine Clark had a similar experience with her 10-year-old and a toy and started Build-a-Bear Workshop.
- When Sara Blakely couldn't find panty hose without seams that didn't bunch up in the Florida humidity, she started Spanx.

All I did was . . .

36

What Happens When You Pivot and No One Notices?

WHEN WE LOOK at pulse, each of the pulse points are opportunities. Sometimes, the interaction is so good or bad that the line changes direction, or pivots. We define *pivot* as a point of decision where an individual decides to make a choice that redefines his or her relationship with a brand—for better or for worse.

Companies can also pivot. For a company, these are the changes in direction that become brand defining. Moving in a new direction can be a scary thing. It can also be what defines the brands that survive and those that don't.

When I was a teenager, in every convenience store you were sure to find two things: more teenagers and a pile of AutoTrader magazines on AutoTrader-branded racks. When a car meant freedom and you only had a limited budget, the newspaper pages were filled with possibilities. If you wanted to sell a car, you'd have to get your ad and picture in before noon Saturday and then it would appear in the weekly magazine.

So when I was speaking in Atlanta at AutoTrader's conference and met the senior vice president at Cox AutoTrader.com, Ian MacDonald, the first thing I said to him was how I loved the magazine.

"Yeah, we stopped printing those. They haven't been on shelves for years."

Well, that was awkward. He went on to tell me that not only had the print division of AutoTrader.com closed down but that, amazingly, no one had even noticed.

Ian MacDonald, who joined AutoTrader.com 11 years ago after working for Ford, for Saab, and overseas in military automotive sales programs, explained to me how the print part of the business had been organized. Each city was its own cost center, with its own printing, ad department, and so on. The whole setup was very old school, like a local newspaper. Over the years, the goal had been to move all these small centers under one central organization to stabilize revenue and rationalize all the hard costs of printing and distribution.

By 2008, the website AutoTrader.com was already a larger business than print—bringing in three times the revenue of the print business. During 2008, the decision was made to begin closing local print shops.

"They weren't doing anything wrong. People just weren't coming in."

Nine months into the process of closing down these centers, the economy crashed. Over the next four months, the print business was shut down completely. The next few years were spent getting advertisers who previously used print to switch to digital. Sales reps from local centers were kept on and retrained for online ads.

By the end of the first quarter of 2009, AutoTrader.com the magazine no longer existed. The racks and displays in stores were left, because it would have been more costly to collect them.

No one called. No one noticed. The entire business just went away, and no one noticed.

What impressed me most about AutoTrader.com was the value it places in data and information. The key wasn't to be in the automotive business; it was to be in the information business. Ian was able to share with me just how much information about the industry they keep track of—and it amazed me. Today, there are four distinct generations in the marketplace, all with purchasing power, and they keep track of their purchasing trends religiously.

They use the data to create the most effective content for their advertisers. For example, their data show a large amount of traffic coming from mobile, and they make sure advertisers know content needs to be mobile-friendly to capture that market. Unlike some other auto sites, Ian told me that AutoTrader.com makes all its money from ad sales, not by taking a cut of any of the auto sales.

AutoTrader.com considers research into the market highly valuable and uses it to position the company as the expert, both to the advertisers and shoppers. By using research, the company makes the market "absolutely predictable." Its relationship to the Manheim Auction company and Kelly Blue Book provides unique insights and knowledge into the entire life of a car.

All this research means that the digital world not only replaced print but improved on it. You can now measure analytics on ads, brands, and specific locations. Salespeople work to educate the dealers on how this information can be used. In today's automotive world, as Ian said, "the dealer doesn't have all the information—the consumer has more." AutoTrader's business has been transformed by this change, because growth needs to depend on demands by the customer.

Closing down a huge part of your brand would be enough to make any company think twice, especially one that had been part of how you got started. Many companies have seen the shift to digital coming and started a website, but most of them are no more than online versions of the print they're already selling. A website shouldn't be only an online brochure. AutoTrader.com has done much more than that. It has moved the cars online—and brought the process of finding one worlds ahead with research.

It's a mistake to think the pivot from print to digital was only about where you read your newspaper. The online world gives opportunities for all kinds of things, and you really can't click your newspaper, no matter what this ad says.

37

Netflix versus Blockbuster

BUSINESSES FAIL ALL the time. I've had a few myself and watched many others. Just about every entrepreneur I know has left one behind. The hardest ones fail slowly, leaving us with some kind of hope that if we'd just tried this or that things would have been different. Ideally, we close up shop with some new lessons learned, only slightly banged up and ready to start again.

When large companies fail, and we certainly have seen some doozies in the past few years, we sit like armchair quarterbacks and make our calls on just what did them in. Of course, if we'd been in charge, we would have seen that whole digital photography thing taking over, right? At times like those, I am thankful to have had my failures quietly and not in the headlines of every newspaper and blog.

The opinions seem to be especially loud when it's a brand we grew up with, was especially successful, or was something that was part of our common experiences. The bigger they are, the harder they fall, right?

Growing up, Friday nights meant wandering the aisles of Blockbuster to pick out a movie—quietly judging other people's choices and hoping you'd remembered your membership card. The kid working behind the counter had seen every movie. The board in the back let you know when *The Crow* would finally be out on video.

Finding a Blockbuster case in the back of your locker at the end of the year and realizing *Monty Python and the Holy Grail* was 9 weeks late . . . the horror.

So, what happened? We are all still watching movies. That hasn't changed. We still spend time Friday nights deciding which ones to watch. Although we all love our headphones, we still enjoy sitting around sharing a movie with our kids and friends. We still exchange currency for movies. Not everything has changed.

We look back now and kind of forget how Blockbuster was once the bad guy, doing in independent community video stores whose staffs really knew about movies and also didn't care if you weren't of age to rent them. Blockbuster wasn't a small town place; it was a big deal to have one close by. The selection at the time was amazing. You could rent video games and consoles there. Tons of movies and snacks were always in stock! All in one place. Blockbuster was convenient and gave us everything we wanted and expected when renting a movie.

Blockbuster didn't change; we did. And that's exactly the problem.

What changed wasn't movies and our want for them. What changed was the format and the expectation of delivery, and Blockbuster didn't keep up. We still want movies. We just don't need the discs anymore, and we expect to be able to sit at home and choose them. We want to choose them from our phones, both when we're home and when we're not. If we want the discs—I have about 300 of them myself[1]—then we order them online and have them delivered to our door the next day. We expect to seamlessly watch a movie on a number of devices now, not just the one TV connected to the one machine.

Blockbuster closed it doors, after many going-out-of-business sales, because it failed to keep up with a change in format and expectation, not because of competitors. Now, that's not to say that it didn't inspire competition. It's known that Reed Hastings, who founded Netflix, started the company—or at least came up with the idea of it—angry about late fees after returning a movie 6 weeks late. All I did after finding my late movie was . . . I coulda been a zillionaire!

---

[1] I hedged my bets and invested in Betamax and then HD-DVD instead of VHS and Blu-ray. That's why this isn't an investment book.

Netflix didn't kill Blockbuster; it just went to where Blockbuster should have gone. Netflix anticipated a change in the way people would be watching media and caught the trend.

Blockbuster was already failing before Netflix was any kind of real competition. "But," as Paula Bernstein wrote, "it looks better to lose a war, than to lose from sheer incompetence."[2]

Sometimes in business, we also just make the wrong choices. In 2000, Blockbuster turned down the option to buy Netflix and instead went into a 20-year deal with a subsidiary of Enron, which filed for bankruptcy the next year. Once Blockbuster saw that Netflix was gaining ground, it entered into the online movie rental market with everything it had left. As the article shows in its awesome info-graphic, in 2004, Reed Hastings told analysts, "in the last six months, Blockbuster has thrown everything but the kitchen sink at us." The next day, Hastings received a package in the mail from Blockbuster: a kitchen sink. Fast shipping and creativity—something Blockbuster may have used better on their rental service . . . but anyway.

Now that Netflix even controls some of the production of content, you can virtually walk in and choose what you want. The content producer, without having advertisements as their profit drive, changed everything. Rather than selling the wrapping, they sell the content. In other industries we see this, too, where books were wrapped in paper and publishers in the paper selling business. Now we no longer need the wrapping. The book is the content—in any format. In music, the content was wrapped in plastic and money made by moving this plastic around and selling it. Now we buy the song or songs. Companies that sold the wrapping die; those that sell the content live. It's as simple as that.

Everyone who watched Blockbuster slowly go out of business had an opinion of what it did wrong—and the truth is, as always, there isn't just one thing. Had Netflix read the trend wrong, we may never have heard of it. Had Blockbuster signed a different deal, we might be paying late fees right now for all the paused episodes of *Mad Men* we're trying to get through.

---

[2] Source: http://bit.ly/1iaQqo1

38

The Secret World of Book Publishing

When I was in eleventh grade, I was called down to the special education office for testing. I'd handed in an English project where we needed to put together a newspaper about Shakespeare. Since I had seen newspapers before, I wrote the project in columns, rather than straight across, like you're reading here. My teacher, it seems, didn't understand the columns and believed me to be entirely illiterate and possibly quite dyslexic, since they read the whole thing straight across. Now while I may have hated Shakespeare, and grade 11 English, I could read and write just fine. After explaining to the special education tester that my writing had been in columns, I was sent back to class . . . a little snarkier from the experience.

If my teacher hadn't been able to see my newspaper columns, I'm very sure he never saw a career path ahead for me that included being a published author.

A lot has changed in the world of writing and publishing since grade 11 English. Today, fewer and fewer people get their news from print newspapers, while online and mobile readership continues to grow.[1] Online readership allows for statistics to be gathered about click-throughs, time spent on different articles and topics, as well as the incorporation of video and links to other resources. News online is much more than a digital copy of the print version. But even with all the options online allows, the news is still the news. The content hasn't changed, just the delivery.

Books are the same. Although publishers and bookstores were once in the paper printing and delivery business, they are now in the business of content. And more and more, the preferred method of content consumption is digital. Amazon now offers books in multiple formats, including print, digital, and audio when available.[2] As an author, I don't care how you consume my content—only that you consume it. I love seeing audiences excited during a keynote and buying my books while I'm still on stage, all from their phones. Whether they buy a digital copy to download or a paper copy to ship to their home or office, the point is that they can now make purchases on the go. And I love it.

Being in the business of paper delivery in books, or plastic delivery in music, movies, and video games, is no longer a model that works in today's digital world. Today, the expectation of delivery is that it be instant.

One of the issues that has arisen with the technological advances that allow this kind of ease of purchase is the belief that because books are now so easy to buy, they should also be so easy to write. Self-published books can be written and made available for sale in a day, complete with homemade covers and little or no editing. I self-published a book myself back in the day, and I have to tell you the process was nothing like writing the books we've written since with our publisher John Wiley & Sons. Can you write an amazing self-published book and make money? Yes. Is publishing dead because this is possible? No. And here's why.

---

[1] Source: http://bit.ly/NewsStats
[2] There isn't an audiobook version of *QR Codes Kill Kittens*, for example, because it's a picture book.

Publishers provide a few important things you probably don't have access to:

1. *Distribution and connection to booksellers and media:* Getting books to stores is no small task. Are you writing a book to increase your consulting business or gain more clients? Because If you are selling books and spending time getting them into stores, that is going to take a lot of time and energy you may not want to spend. Publishers have booths at trade shows and access to bookstores from the local indy in your neighborhood to Barnes and Noble.

2. *Expertise in editing, design, and marketing:* Sure, you can get a book cover designed on Fiverr for $5, but you're going to get what you pay for. Think you know everything about book formatting and editing? Maybe you do, but there's a good chance having someone else's eyes on your creation is only going to make it better. Marketing a book about marketing like I did is one thing, but if your book is about the rainforest or how to be a better photographer, marketing may be better left to the experts. Publishers know how to sell books; it's what they do.

3. *Position as a gatekeeper:* Putting a book, or anything you create, out into the world is a scary thing. That is true whether you publish yours yourself or use a publisher. It's just part of the process. Although self-publishing is gaining more respect as famous authors turn to it, there is still an automatic clout attached to using a publisher. It means someone who knows about books, who makes books for a living, believes yours is good enough. And that still means something.

4. *A platform:* By the time John Wiley & Sons approached me to write a book, I had already built a substantial platform online. I'd spent years building my community and positioning myself as an expert in marketing and social media. I had a well-read newsletter, a consulting and speaking client list, a Twitter following, a busy Facebook page, and a successful blog.

But my publisher was also an amazing resource for learning about the book business. There are so many books published every year. According to Jack Covert from 1800CEORead, about 11,000 business books alone each year. That isn't counting self-published e-books, the numbers of which just keep growing. That means your book is coming out in a sea of other titles, and you need to do everything you can to distinguish yourself.

When a book first comes out people don't realize the payola[3] involved with getting a spot on the shelves. Front shelves, circular tables, even spots at the end of rows are all for sale. Placement is very valuable in such a saturated market. We learned quickly with *UnMarketing* the value of the preorder. Having orders ready to go when the book officially launches means they will all go through at once—pushing your book into the best-selling lists. This push can happen before anyone has even had your book in hand to read it, changing the value of the best-seller title to one of marketing, not necessarily quality.

The title of best-seller is now so important to authors that they will do whatever it takes to reach the list. There are programs where an author can pay to have large quantities of books purchased as preorders or on release to grab a best-seller list spot.

Here are five types of best-sellers you need to know about:

1. *Long-lasting legits:* Having a book on shelves past a few months is an accomplishment, let alone having a book that stays on a best-selling list. These are books that people love, even after they've read them. Here the term *best-seller* means what it should: most-loved.
2. *The best-selling spike:* These are the ones that have paid to be here, or at the very least planned some well-timed preorders. I don't see anything wrong with these, but if they immediately drop off the radar as soon as people start actually consuming the content, that means they didn't really earn the best-selling title.
3. *The Amazon spike:* Amazon keeps an up-to-date list of best-sellers in each of its gazillion categories. If you want to be the best-selling book about giraffes that like travel on a Thursday at 2:20 AM, then this is the ticket! Now, please understand, if you've written a book and it hits a best-selling list on Amazon, you should be excited; it's a huge accomplishment, and you deserve some cheers and high fives.

---

[3] A music industry term for the illegal pay for play of music on the radio.

But I don't think these 5 minutes spent on a best-seller list mean you can add it to your bio and book jacket.

4. *Free "best selling":* Best selling is two words, and the second one is *selling,* which means someone needed to exchange currency for your book. You cannot claim to have a more successful book than ones that cost money when you're giving it away for free . . . you just can't. Authors do this by offering a free Kindle edition of their book for 48 hours.

5. *My best-selling book:* And we've reached the bottom. I've seen more than a few authors making this claim, and when I questioned how their book was a best-seller, this was their answer:

"Well, Scott, I've written three books, and this is my best-selling one!"

And that ladies and gentlemen is the book industry.

39

Crowdfunding

YOU MAY NOT know this about me, but I'm a documentary movie producer. As a huge documentary fan, my iPad is filled with them for travel—funding a movie was an investment in something I love. I've also backed products like a 3D doodler, an iPhone stand, and a cartoon about Paco the Judo Popcorn.

Sites like Kickstarter and Indiegogo have made it possible for everyone to be backers and for many a company to get off the ground. Today, it seems all we need is an idea and a catchy video to get the idea shared, and we're ready to get crowdfunded!

Here is why I fund projects:

1. People I know, like, and trust have funded them first. I know this because I've linked these sites with my Facebook account, and they let me know whenever friends back projects.
2. Projects interest me: documentaries, tech, nonprofits.
3. Incentives.

Some sites set a minimum amount that must be raised for the project to go ahead, whereas others send whatever money is funded along to the project owners. The idea of setting a minimum is to test the viability of the project: If the amount isn't met, you need to listen to that response from your market.

There are pros and cons to both ways of raising money. One interesting point to remember is that if potential donors' money is not returned for unsuccessfully funded projects, they may never donate again.[1]

In a very young industry of online crowdfunding, trust is still being built, and I think keeping donors happy is going to be critical in whether or not these sites are still as successful in the future.

Kickstarter, for example, does not provide any kind of support to backers once the money is in the hands of the project team. So please remember when you send money through the site that you are making an investment, not purchasing an incentive. If you are in it for the iPod mini or copy of the book when it comes out, just go and buy those. Don't invest more than you can afford to lose.

These projects and products are usually only in their infancy, and things often do not quite go according to plan. If you are considering setting up a campaign for yourself, remember that, as always in business, communication is so important. If products are late, good communication can save a project from becoming a bad kind of famous. Like the Lockitron, for example, which still hasn't shipped its product to most of the backers of the $2.2 million campaign.[2]

To let you know a little more about crowdfunding and Kickstarter specifically, I looked to an expert on the topic, Jason Sadler.[3] He wrote one of my favorite posts on the subject:

> If you're looking for the perfect success story for how to dominate Kickstarter and get your project fully funded, look no further than Web Smith and Kevin Lavelle from Mizzen+Main. If you've ever thought about doing a crowdfunding project, follow every move they made (and steal with pride!). This applies to Kickstarter, Indiegogo, other crowdfunding platforms, and even product launches on your own website.

[1] Source: http://bit.ly/1iaPVdl
[2] Source: http://tcrn.ch/1iT1ou1
[3] JasonDoesStuff.com

The Mizzen+Main Kickstarter project . . . launched yesterday at 8am. At 1pm yesterday it was already over 100% funded. As of publishing this blog post, they've raised $28,000+ and have almost doubled their goal in just 24 hours. This definitely isn't the norm with most crowdfunding projects, but here are some of the reasons I believe their Kickstarter project was such an "overnight success" and yours can be too.

They Built a Solid Brand

But, Jason, I'm starting my brand with Kickstarter. I want the world to meet me for the first time through my crowdfunding campaign. WRONG. No you don't. And you know why? Because only about 0.001 percent of crowdfunding projects have zero existing brand, launch a crowdfunding campaign, and have it turn out to be successful. You want to have a much better shot at being successful, right? Work on building a solid brand first like Mizzen+Main did (two and half years of work). They have a great logo, have an easy-to-use website, have sold products and received feedback from users, are active on social media, and . . .

They Built a Customer Base

This sounds counterintuitive, right? You're thinking about using Kickstarter so you can build your first customer base. WRONG. Again, if you don't have an existing brand, your barrier to entry is huge when it comes to crowdfunding. Even the Kickstarter FAQ says that "*the majority of funding initially comes from the fans and friends of each project.*" If you want to hedge your bets with your crowdfunding project, and you should, build a customer base first and then use a platform like Kickstarter as a marketing tool.

They Built Relationships

Full disclosure, I've known Web Smith from Mizzen+Main since 2011. We met playing pickup basketball at SXSW and have

(continued)

(*continued*)

stayed in touch ever since. We've both had other projects, have been busy, and had our own lives, but we've stayed connected. When the Mizzen+Main Kickstarter launched, Web shared it with me and I immediately backed it. Honestly, I didn't need any of Mizzen+Main's awesome-looking shirts or the cool-looking 0–5 Blazer, but I believe in Web and wanted to support him in any way I could. I'm sure Web and Kevin both reached out to their friends when the project kicked off. I did the same thing when I launched SponsorMyBook. There were about 30 to 50 people that I e-mailed before the SponsorMyBook website went live, and I shared the project with them. Why? Because . . .

They Got Momentum Going Early

A quick stat directly from Kickstarter: 80 percent of projects that raised more than 20 percent of their goal were successfully funded. By getting some early momentum, it shows other potential backers that they should also back the project. It's the same thing bartenders do at bars and restaurants. They do what's called stuffing the tip jar—and they stuff it with their own money. Now when customers arrive, it already looks like people have tipped them, so they feel compelled to tip as well. Haven't you ever seen an empty tip jar and thought, "Hmm . . . I don't want to be the first or only person to tip these people. Why hasn't anyone else?" After that, you start to wonder about the quality of product or service being offering. Early momentum is key with any project launch and should be a big part of your planning.

IMPORTANT: They Had a Realistic Funding Goal

All too often people start Kickstarter campaigns with incredibly lofty funding goals: $10,000, $40,000, $100,000! Kickstarter says that out of 55,815 successfully funded projects, 48,949 of them raised $19,999 or less. And out of those 48,949 projects, 41,485 of them had funding goals of $9,999 or less. As soon as your goal exceeds $10,000, your chances of getting successfully funded decrease greatly. And if your goal is more than $20,000, your chances are extremely low. The point here is that although you may want to raise $50,000 or $100,000, you should start with the *absolute* bare minimum (and I mean minimum) amount of money you need to get your project going. My good buddy Clay Hebert is a crowdfunding expert who has helped 33 crowdfunding projects raise nearly $3 million. I'd highly recommend signing up for his upcoming Crowdfunding Hacks course if you're thinking about crowdfunding.

They Got Press Early

This goes along with getting momentum and building relationships. Media folks like talking about things that are interesting. If your crowdfunding project helps them write a great story that gets shared, it's a win for them. And, if they write about your crowdfunding project and it gets fully funded (or way overfunded), they look good for writing about it early. Reach out to any press contacts you may have, and share your crowdfunding project. It's especially good timing if you do it after the first day when you have some solid momentum rolling (go get 'em, Web and Kevin!).

They Spent Time/Money on an Awesome Video!

I've watched countless Kickstarter and Indiegogo videos that were just plain awful. Kickstarter is not the place you should be sharing the first video you've ever been in or ever filmed and edited. I completely understand if you're bootstrapping and can't spend thousands of dollars on video production. However, you can find college kids at a local university who are budding videographers and looking for work to practice on. And hey, if you want to film it yourself, that's totally fine; just practice, practice, practice, and practice more. Get incredibly comfortable with what you're saying and watch your video with other people to get their real reactions. If they get uncomfortable watching you, why was it? What can you learn from their feedback? Personally, I would look

(continued)

(*continued*)

at the cost of your Kickstarter video as part of the initial amount of money you're trying to raise. If you watched Mizzen+Main's video, I think you'll agree that it was money incredibly well spent!

(Side note: If you watch, you will notice in the Mizzen+Main Kickstarter video that they didn't say "Hello, Kickstarter!" Be unique. Be original. People already know they're on Kickstarter watching you talk to them; it isn't mandatory to say "Hello, Kickstarter.")

They Offered a Great Product

Mizzen+Main did a brilliant thing by *not* doing a Kickstarter project two years ago when they first started their men's clothing company. Instead, they spent two-plus years creating products and learning along the way. I bet even Kevin and Web would admit that the first products they made weren't perfect and needed tweaking and redoing. Whatever the product is that you're trying to get funding for, make sure it's something great. And like any business or product you sell, it helps if your product solves a problem.

Then, Make Sure You Deliver

I backed a project on Kickstarter in December 2012, and I still haven't received the product. This seems to be a common theme with Kickstarter projects, especially tech-related ones. While I'm trying to be patient and understanding, I'm always wondering why it's taking so long. Will I ever get the product? It may not seem like a huge deal to make your customers wait, but I'd be willing to bet a customer that gets the product they backed in a timely fashion is way more likely to purchase more products from that company and be a brand evangelist. I'm not even going to share the project I backed on Kickstarter in December because I'm so bummed at this point that it's taken this long. I know a lot of people feel the same way about the Lockitron project.

I'm sure Mizzen+Main will deliver rewards to their backers in a very timely fashion, just based on their reputation.

My hat goes off to Web and Kevin. Not only have they built a business doing what they love, they've created a loyal customer base that was primed and ready to support their Kickstarter project. Learn from what they've done, and don't go all-or-nothing on crowdfunding. Put in the work ahead of time and use crowdfunding as a marketing tool that can also generate revenue and build your customer list.

Jason really knows his stuff! Before you get started on your crowdfunding campaign, do your research. The online world is filled with stories of crowdfunding disasters for you to learn from and avoid the same mistakes. Some of the common ones are not having your manufacturing set up, forgetting about shipping and other fulfillment costs, and jumping ahead to buyers, leaving your funders behind, empty-handed, and angry about it.

On the other hand, crowdsfunding is an incredible opportunity to reach potential customers and the sales cloud. By gaining interest and investment from fans early—both financial and emotional—you get a head start on UnSelling.

40

Customer Reviews

The Good, the Bad, and the Future

The Good

Trusted referrals have always been the gold of marketing. The online world didn't create the value of opinions of friends and family. For as long as we can remember, "I know a guy for that" economies have run successfully off referrals. Referrals from people we know, like, and trust are so valuable that larger companies and the online market have been trying to copy the kind of community and connection once reserved for local businesses.

Online reviews are making that real for companies all over the world. When I'm looking for a product or service, I want to know if anyone I already know, like, and trust has used it and what they thought. So having great online reviews is tremendously powerful, especially when they come through trusted communities like Facebook.

As we saw in the sales cloud chapter, 60 percent of sales decisions are made before a company has any direct contact with you. This is where reviews live—where the opinions of customers past can come back to haunt a brand's future. We trust people more than brands, especially when it comes to brand experiences.

The hierarchy of reviews looks like this:

- Review from a friend or family member that you trust.
- Review from the masses. Online sites such as Yelp rely on a large number of reviews painting a picture of what a place is like. The more reviews, the less valuable a one-off experience is, and the more reliable the opinion should be.
- Advertisement or bottom-of-the-barrel success. Here we see brand messages, commercials, and sites tuned for search engine optimization (SEO) to make sure the company's products or services come up first when you Google.

This past year, Alison and I took our podcast live and did a panel at New Media Expo in Las Vegas. To add to the awesome, and to fill the early morning room, we promised to have donuts to go along with the awesome. Although we consider ourselves Vegas locals, we had never visited a donut shop in town. We headed out that morning and decided to search Yelp.com for donut shops and see what we could find.

We figured something would pop up, or at least we'd find the local Dunkin' Donuts . . .

What we found as the second entry in the list was Ronald's Donuts, with 4.5 stars and a whopping 416 reviews! If you don't use Yelp often, you need to know that is a ton of reviews for any spot, let alone a privately owned donut shop—which turned out to be in a mini-mall beside a tarot reader.

We were sold and headed over. Reviews were all amazing and made suggestions regarding which donuts we should try. The site gave us all the info we needed: hours, price, and that we needed to grab some money because credit and debit cards were not accepted for payment. The panel and the donuts were a huge hit, and we plan on going back for the apple turnovers, which we hear are a must-try. Ronald's is known as a spot for Vegan[1] treats as well, in case you're out that way and need a snack.

The Bad

Fighting the good fight in the land of online reviews can be challenging for businesses. We all want a chance to set things right, and it's

---

[1] Amazingly, *Vegan* is not a person from Vegas, but it should be.

hard to know a customer was unhappy and went online to voice his opinion—sometimes, but not always, in lieu of letting you know in person. We are passive in person and aggressive online, and as a business owner that can hurt. And sometimes deciding what to do with that defensiveness leads owners down a dangerous road.

People have been sued for negative reviews, and there can be a backlash to companies when they sue, regardless of whether they win or lose. Reviewers have been sued for writing bad reviews about everything from contractors to nail salons.

As written in the *Washington Post*:

> Lawyers say it is one of a growing number of defamation lawsuits over online reviews on sites such as Yelp, Angie's List and Trip-Advisor and over Internet postings in general. They say the freewheeling and acerbic world of Web speech is colliding with the ever-growing importance of online reputations for businesses, doctors, restaurants, even teachers.
>
> It's snark vs. status.[2]

Reviewers see it as their right to share bad products and service, and companies feel it is their right to defend online reputations. Reviews can be shared and live forever online.

A 2011 Harvard study quantified just how big an effect those negative Yelp postings can have: A one-star increase among reviews of Seattle restaurants led to a 5 to 9 percent growth in revenue. That's just a one-star improvement. That's the power of the sales cloud.

The threat of a lawsuit is often enough to quiet angry reviewers. Here is one question asked on TripAdvisor, another site where reviews are king:

How do I contact Tripadvisor? I posted a review for a hotel that lied to me and changed rates after I booked a room. I canceled the room and posted a review (approved by Tripadvisor) clearly stating my experience and that I had not stayed at

[2]Source: http://bit.ly/SuedForReviews

the hotel. I have a clear email chain with the hotel documenting everything.

It seems to me that Trip Advisor should help users out when owners threaten to sue over reviews. Please advise.

Thank you.

Someone from TripAdvisor support gave the following reply:

First, Trip Advisor does not offer one-on-one telephone or email support.

Second, Trip Advisor is not in a position to offer legal advice or support. The comments in your review are your subjective opinion of the property.

Your "approved by Tripadvisor" review was approved only on the basis that it met the guidelines for posting a review, not on the content of the review itself.

Respectfully, IMO, many less than scrupulous managers and owners have resorted to scare tactics to have less than favourable reviews removed by the writer (you). That is because TripAdvisor will not delete a review, if disputed by the hotel, just because it is negative in tone.[3]

Whether you agree with TripAdvisor's stance on the matter or not, staying neutral with respect to the content of a review is probably the best stance for it to take. TripAdvisor isn't in the business of sending employees to check up on locations; the site is crowdsourced, and to encourage openness you need to let people share.

The Future

In 2013, an investigation into the writing of fake reviews on Yelp called Operation Clean Turf "caught 19 different companies, most of

---

[3]Source: http://bit.ly/TripAdvisorHelp

them SEO (search engine optimization) or reputation management firms for hire, that were writing fake reviews for small businesses that paid them." Yelp had known about the investigation and cooperated. Fake reviews left unstopped would destroy the value of review sites.

To keep out fake reviews, Yelp uses a filter that "weeds out 25% of reviews posted. That does not mean that 25% of reviews are fake, but that 25% of reviews are either suspect or simply less helpful. Still, it is a surprisingly large portion. And a study conducted in April by Maritz Research found that, of 3,400 people (an admittedly small sample size) who use review sites like Yelp, in most cases only half of them trust the reviews they're seeing (59% on TripAdvisor and Zagat, 53% on Yelp). The study's results suggest that consumer trust in user-generated reviews is eroding."[4]

This is why sites like TripAdvisor have added the option for users to connect the site to Facebook—because, as we said at the start, reviews by friends and family are trusted more than those of the masses. This same added trust creation is happening on crowdfunding sites like Kickstarter as well, where trust is the most valuable commodity the site has to offer.

So how do we get good reviews for our products and services? Well, first, we need to start with something worth talking about. Reviews can only amplify customer experience; they can't change it. Second, ask for them. Not in a skeezy way or a pushy way, but let customers know that their opinions are of value to you. If you check out my speaking page, www.ScottStratten.com, you will see testimonials from keynote clients, many of which we asked for. It's not that we needed to beg for them; its just that people are so busy with everything going on, that even the most ecstatic customer may need to be asked for a review.

A great example of how to ask for a review happened to me in my home away from home, Las Vegas. I'm going to admit I was nervous, and I wasn't even the one driving. We had finally done it. We had rented sports cars to drive in the desert, a bucket list item for most stereotypical guys out there.

My buddy Steve and I were sitting in the waiting room of World Class Driving in Las Vegas, getting psyched to drive an assortment of Ferraris and Lamborghinis toward Red Rock. I would be riding shotgun,

[4]Source: http://bit.ly/FakeYelp

because I don't know the difference between torque and a fork.[5] One of the main people in charge was going through very important things like safety and driving etiquette while in Las Vegas. The only other thing he brought up was TripAdvisor, and it was brief and awesome. He said:

> If you love your experience with us today, please leave us a review on TripAdvisor.com. If you didn't love your experience with us, please come to me immediately and I promise to make it right.

He then handed out postcards with the TripAdvisor URL and World Class Driving page. He knew how important good reviews were and how many people who leave bad ones wouldn't say anything until after they left, so he opened the door to remedy anything less than five stars.

Alison and I have been to dozens of attractions in Vegas. We run the Vegas 30 podcast[6] for people over 30. (Too old to stand in line, too young to retire to the bingo hall.) And this is the only time we've ever heard of any place mentioning an online review. There is a huge weight for any tourism attraction when it comes to online review sites, yet almost every place fails to mention them at all. They just hope people leave good ones.

World Class Driving is always near or at the top of the "Things to Do" list on TripAdvisor for Las Vegas.[7] In fact, as of this writing, it's number three.

Online reviews are here to stay. Whether it's passive venting on Twitter or posting your experience to friends on Facebook, when you get a bunch of people together as a community, we talk. I love the new power consumers have today and believe anything that keeps companies focused on their quality and service is for the good. Does that mean I haven't read a book review that hurt my heart? Of course not. But I believe if we do good work, it will speak for itself. The majority of our customers just want to receive what they were expecting: quality and service. Focus on that, rather than scrounging the Internet for negative reviews, and your reputation will represent that good work.

---

[5] You could say my tires needed to be filled with more efficient air, and I wouldn't be able to argue.
[6] www.TheVegas30.com
[7] http://bit.ly/UnClassy

41

Beware of Mountain Climbers Who Sell Equipment

PICTURE A SUCCESSFUL mountain climber standing on the summit. Exhausted and exhilarated, but if he gets his arm caught in a crevice, he may have a book/movie deal waiting.

With success come people who want to learn about the climber's strategy. What equipment did he use? How did he pace the ascent? These are the so-called best practices we look for in business.

What if this climber, instead of listing all his equipment and strategies, threw all of the stuff off the other side of the mountain and said, "You don't need anything! Except my new book/course/consulting: 'How to Climb to the Summit of Success.'"[1]

It's become the thing to do these days: Throw away what got you to where you are and morph your experiences into something that you can market and sell to others. Best-selling authors tell you that you don't need a publisher when their original publisher was one of the most important reasons they have their sizeable platform in the first place.

---

[1]Damn, that's gold. I need to write that.

Actors crowdfund movies and say you don't need a studio when without the studio-produced sitcom, they wouldn't have raised $5, because no one would have known who they were.

It has become way too easy for today's experts and successes to ignore the tools that took them up the mountain and instead sell us "five easy steps to success" in their place. There is no such thing as an easy trip to the top without hard work, luck, and a whole lot of tools.

This happens all the time in the world of social media. I've seen a lot of very successful "big names" in social who have then dropped tens of thousands of followers, even though many of these followers had been a part of their success in the first place, and sometimes only followed them in the first place in reciprocation of the original connection. Users with huge followings only need to keep up with replies for social media success, but for a new user that will lead to dead air online.

Success in social media can be measured in a bunch of different ways. For an entrepreneur, it may be finding his or her water cooler online or connecting with his or her marketplace. Success doesn't need to be measured in numbers, but rather in the quality of the connections. That said, having a large platform will amplify your message and allow it to reach more people. Once you have that platform, it is too easy to make how you get the word out about your business seem as though it could be duplicated by someone without that platform. Other things someone on top of the mountain may have besides the audience could include a team of people to share the work, confidence from past successes, recognition as an expert in the field, and the trust that comes with that position. If you want to learn from those at the top, find out what tools they used when they were climbing—not just the tools that are working for them now that they're at the top.

The view is different from the top of the mountain. Your connections are different, your credibility is different, and the size of your platform is different. I wrote in *UnMarketing* that you can't learn from millionaires, and this is one step up from there. Although I love retrospective advice, where we look back and share how we would have climbed the mountain differently, we need to be careful to start where our followers are and be honest about what tools they are going to need for success. And please, take extra care when the climber on the top of the mountain says the only way up is to buy a tool kit with his name on it, because that's the worst advice of all.

In the next few chapters, we're going to look at tools for UnSelling and how you can use them to move the pulse of your customers, create awesome content for the sales cloud, and generally be better at business.

42

Social Media by the Dozen

IN *UNMARKETING*, we went through some of the basics on the biggies in social media sites: Twitter, Facebook, and LinkedIn.[1] When we talk about UnSelling, social media is a powerful tool to listen and connect. It's just that: a tool—like your website or your phone. Awesome things can happen in business, and sometimes those happen through social media sites.

Social Media Explained by @EliLanger on Twitter

Twitter: I'm eating a #donut.

Facebook: I like donuts.

Foursquare: This is where I eat donuts.

Instagram: Here is a vintage photo of my donut.

(continued)

---

[1]Some sites to check out are SocialMediaExplorer.com, SocialMediaExaminer.com, and Mashable.com

(*continued*)

YouTube: Here I am eating a donut.

LinkedIn: My skills include donut eating.

Pinterest: Here's a donut recipe.

MySpace: I'm eating a donut alone.

Spotify: Now listening to "donuts."

Google+: I'm a Google employee who eats donuts.

Reddit: I'm eating a donut. AMA.

Vine: I'm eating a donut . . . I'm eating a donut . . . I'm eating a donut.

Snapchat: My donut will disappear in 5 seconds.

Jelly: Does anyone know where I can get a donut?

There are new sites every day. Some grow to become user favorites, habitual stops during their day to share, connect, and learn. Others come and go just as quickly.

Your market is there. If your niche market includes humans, they are using social media. From millennials to our moms, people are online being social every day. And they are talking about your product or services, your competitors, and your industry. You can either be a part of the conversation or not.

When setting up your website, remember to make sharing your content on these sites easy. For the UnPodcast, we use a button that tweets a set line from the episode with every share.

Just be sure not to include too many icons. I once went to share a post and it had no less than 250 sharing options. Check out the pic:

Bookmark & Share

http://www.citynews.ca/2014/02/18/the-inside-story-the-brampton-bakery...

http://www.citynews.ca/2014/02/18/the-inside-story-the-brampton-bakery-that...

100zakladok	2 Tag	2linkme
A97abi	Adfty	Adifni
ADV QR code	Amazon	Amen Me!
Aol Lifestream	AOL Mail	APSense
Arto	Azadegi	Baang
Baidu	BallTribe	Beat100
BiggerPockets	Bit.ly	bizSugar
Bland takkinn	Blinklist	Blip
Blogger	Bloggy	Blogkeen
Blogmarks	Blurpalicious	Bobrdobr
BonzoBox	BookmarkingNet	Bookmarky.cz
Bookmerken	Box.net	Brainify
Bryderi	BuddyMarks	Buffer
Buzzzy	Camyoo	Care2
Cherry Share	Chime.In	Chiq
Cirip	CiteULike	ClassicalPlace
CleanPrint	CleanSave	Cndig
Colivia.de	Communicate	COSMiQ
CSS Based	Curate.Us	Delicious
DigaCultura	Digg	Diggita
Digo	Diigo	doMelhor
Dosti	DotNetShoutout	Douban
Draugiem.lv	Dropjack	Dudu
dzone	edelight	EFactor
eKudos	elefanta.pl	Email
Email App	Embarkons	Evernote
extraplay	EzySpot	Fab Design
Fabulously40	Facebook	Fai Informazione
Fancy	Fark	Farkinda
Fashiolista	FAVable	Fave
favlog	Favoriten.de	Favoritus

It was so overdone, I ended up sharing a picture of the share buttons instead of the post! The scary thing is, this is only a third of the actual image! It would have taken four pages of this book to show the entire thing.

UnSelling means focusing on the product and experiences first, social media second. If you make your customers happy, they will rule social media for you. They will spread the word and jump to your defense when things go wrong.

That said, social media is where we go to vent, and hearing these passive conversations about your company or industry is invaluable. If you have time to answer your customer service phone calls, then why shouldn't you have time to reply to a tweet about your product or service? It is just too easy for companies to blame all their problems on social media today when really social media isn't at fault at all.

Here are a few things in business that are definitely *not* social media problems:

1. People complaining about your product online is not a social media problem.

    "Scott, we have a problem with social media. People keep going on there and complaining about our products. We just don't know what to do!"[2]

    Well, for starters, how about you make a better product.

    This is a quality problem. Social media can't make your horrible product better. And keeping people from talking about just how bad it is can't be fixed with a social media strategy. If you want people to say good things about your company, go ahead and run a great company.

2. No one replying to your Facebook invite is not a social media problem.

    "Scott, I just don't understand why no one replied to our invite for an untargeted (geographically or topically) event that we sent out to 2,000+ people we took no time to get to know."

    Clearly Facebook is broken.

3. Customers sharing their terrible experience at your restaurant is not a social media problem.

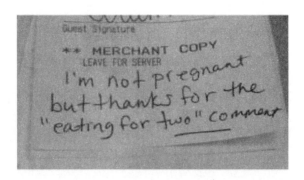

---

[2]Someone actually stood up during a talk and made this statement—in front of an audience.

A little advice I like to share from stage: "Listen closely. Never, ever assume she's pregnant. Unless she tells you to your face. Or you can see the head."

This is a rudeness problem.

4. No one commenting on your blog isn't a social media problem.

What are you writing about? If your blog is a glorified brochure, no one is going to read it, let alone comment. You need to think about your audience and what they want to read. Of course you want to share your newest sale or product launch, but why should they care?

Have you grown a platform? The online world is a busy place. Getting one comment means you have 100 times that in readership. Focus on getting the readers first, write about something they care about and you are passionate about, and comments will come.

Seriously. How hard have you made it to comment? Are your comments moderated? How much information does someone need to give to leave one? If you have people reading your blog, you shouldn't make it hard for them to comment.

5. Sending out a tweet like this isn't a social media problem.

City of Vaughan
@City_of_Vaughan

Everyone on my street has double gararges...who are these ⬛cknuts who don't put their car in the garage when we get 2 feet of snow? #dumb

2013-02-08 7:23 AM

41 RETWEETS **11** FAVORITES

This is a hiring problem. Time and time again we hear about how important it is to "implement a strict social media policy." You have hired these people right? They didn't just stumble in off the street and start tweeting on your behalf. Why would you want someone who would speak this way about your constituency working in your office?

Hire fewer morons, and the percentage of mistweets will decrease. How's that for a policy?

6. No one replying to your tweets isn't a social media problem.

   If you walked into a room full of people and started talking, didn't care about what anyone else was saying, or why they were there—you just walked around shouting—how do you think that would go?

   If you don't spend time replying and talking with people on social, no one is going to take the time to reply to you. That is the secret of social media. Treat it the way you would an in-person networking event.

   "Twitter is a conversation, not a dictation."—Scott Stratten.

   (Also don't quote yourself. No one likes that.)

7. Your public relations (PR) campaign falling flat isn't a social media problem.

   Working with bloggers and social media people is an art, and some people are really good at it. For every person who is, there are about three dozen who aren't. We get a lot of flack for focusing only on negative PR stories, but it's almost impossible not to.

   When you e-mail me looking for someone to test out your women's athletic gear, you may have the wrong person.

   And when someone says no thanks, remember to stop trying the same stuff. It's not anyone's job to delete your bad PR e-mails. It is your job not to send them.

8. The world finding out your company employs morons isn't a social media problem.

So the employee in question is "in the process of being fired." Taco Bell issued a statement that the photo was taken as part of an internal contest and that the shells were never served to any actual customers.

This is a communication problem between the company and the individual who shared the photo (violating the companies social media policies). Or it's a hiring problem. *Or* it's simply horrible taste. But either way, social media is a tool. And so is this guy.

43

What Really Matters in Social

THE TERM SOCIAL is a pretty basic one. It means the interaction between people. That's it. Remember when you fled to the basement during family gatherings and your mom would come downstairs and ask you to come up and "be social"? [1]

That's all I've ever asked of people who use social media: Just be social.

Come up for a bit, show your face, and talk to the company that's come to visit.

I've been screaming out against automation and scheduling in social since 2008. I've been singing the same song for more than six years, which is how I assume Lynyrd Skynyrd feels like every time people yell out "Freebird!" from the crowd—only slightly less cool.

Success in social has always been simple. If you wanted to use social media, just show up and be social.

Somewhere along the way, we made it okay to have a presence online without actually being present. On Twitter, for example,

---

[1] Just me? Come on. Not even during Thanksgiving when Uncle Larry hit the sauce and started telling awkward jokes?

we went from a site filled with people there because they wanted to connect with other like-minded users to people there because they "had to." With more and more users, the possibility of profiting from connections changed the very nature of what made the site great. Now Twitter was too big to ignore. We had to get our message, our content and our products in front of all those eyes. It was time to scale it, grow it, blast it.

Along came scheduling software, and I screamed about how bad it was for Twitter. People screamed back, and it was a party!

Then the hybrid schedulers came out. They were a kinder, gentler scheduler.

"Yes," they'd say, "we schedule, but we also have notifications set up, so if someone replies to the scheduled tweet, we see it, and reply! Ta-da! Automated engagement! Take that, Stratten!"

This was where the last nail in the coffin happened for me on Twitter in my hopes it would ever go back to a wonderful place to network. You see, the problem with this fantasy of scheduling yet listening for your name is the exact thing that is bringing down social media. You're only listening when someone calls *your* name. Social, especially Twitter, cannot survive on selfish social practices. Social is give and take: I listen to you; you listen to me. It's not just about replying. It's about replying and connecting when the original message wasn't directed only at you.

You can't just sit in the basement and wait for people to call your name to engage. You need to be replying to conversations that aren't just about you.

Twitter is imploding as a conversational site. Brands listen only for their name, and people automate Facebook and Instagram posts, because heck, the world needs to see your smoothie pics—and they need to see them on every platform possible. I've seen a lot of the big players on Twitter fall into this trap. And one of the worst culprits was me.

Yep. Yours truly, the preacher of the conversation, the most popular Canadian if it wasn't for Bieber on Twitter. I realized I had become exactly what I hated. [2] I preached on stage and in previous books that Twitter was a conversation, not a dictation, trumpeting my "80 percent

---

[2] I can hear Obi-Wan Kenobi yelling, "YOU WERE THE CHOSEN ONE!!!"

of my tweets are replies!" to everyone who would listen . . . but there was a catch.

I've tweeted more than 100,000 times, meaning 80,000+ have been replies, but there were two types: active replies and reactive replies. Active replies were what I did in the beginning: seeking out tweets in the main feed of others and replying to them. They weren't directed at me specifically, just 140 characters put out into the cyber system, yearning for a reply. That's how Twitter was built. Someone tweeted something, and we replied! Reactive replies are what I did once I became "popular." I looked only at my "@ replies" column, and replied to only those that spoke directly to me.

My intentions were good, for the most part. I didn't want to miss a tweet someone directed at me. I had written multiple books about being social, and I'd be dammed if I was going to miss a tweet from a reader, since half the time they'd send me a tweet to see if I would walk my talk, like I was some sort of dancing monkey on the pier working for nickels. I didn't check my following feed, because I was busy! Sheesh! But that's the problem. Have you ever met that person at a function who talked only about themselves? Ya, that's me. And you. And anyone who replies only when replied to.

I still don't understand scheduling tweets at all. I know your justifications for it: You have multiple accounts, you have something that *has* to go out, and you may be busy, blah, blah. But I ask you this: What is so important that it *must* go out at a specific time but not important enough for you to be there to send it?

Social works only when we interact with one another. The downfall of social is real and it's happening, and that's sad that I, and some of you, weren't listening to hear it when it started. Let's turn it around.

44

Who Polices the Police Presentations?

ETHICS AND DISCLOSURE can get a little fuzzy online. It's so much easier to present ourselves as more or less or even just different from how we really are. From our perfectly lit profile pictures, to the products we're paid to promote, to all those gym workouts someone else is posting every day, the Internet gives us a lot of opportunities to be a little less ethical than we might be face to face.

While awaiting my turn on stage to keynote a broadcasting conference, the speaker preceding me was from the government body that regulates content. You know the one: They make sure everything is on the up and up, that everyone stays within the law. They're the police of the airways, if I may.

He starts his presentation using a typical stock photo of someone on a cell phone to show he's a technology expert, of course. The photo is so overused. It's familiar enough that the audience recognizes it right away—no doubt they would be seeing it a few times during the conference.

Unfortunately, this is not a story about bad stock photos. This is a story about ethics, and the behavior of someone meant to police ethics in others.

The photo, larger than life up on the screen, had a giant watermark over it—the watermark that stock photo sites put on their images to keep people from stealing them. The ethics expert had stolen the picture and proceeded to put it into his ethics presentation.

I was entirely speechless.

Maybe I could have let it go as a brain fart if it was a one-time occurrence as his talked opened. But for the next 15 slides of his presentation, it was watermark after watermark. I texted Alison from the audience in awe and kept repeating to myself, "Don't bring this up on stage. Don't bring this up on stage . . . "

I'm pretty proud of my self-control actually. I brought it up only twice.

If the governing body in charge of ethics cannot be ethical, what hope do the rest of us have?

When we live and work in a world where things posted online live forever, we need to act accordingly. How this person chose to create his presentation went much further than the room we stood in. But like all things in social, the point isn't the amplification through media; it's the fact that he thought stealing photos and using them in a presentation was okay. Start with ethical behavior, and social will never be a problem for you. Don't want to get caught up in an online scandal? Don't act scandalously. Afraid of the geekalanche reaction to a prejudice tweet? Start by checking your prejudices and attitudes.

45

How Not to Apologize

THIS SHOULD REALLY be Humanity 101. We teach kids in kindergarten how to do it for goodness' sake. But over and over again I am amazed by just how horrible we are at making an apology. We all make mistakes, and the world of social media can certainly amplify them, but, as we spoke about in *The Book of Business Awesome/UnAwesome*, when it hits the fan, it isn't time to hide behind the fan. It's time to be awesome—or at the very least, genuinely sorry.

Step 1: Social Media Fark Up

"All tweets are my own."

This is the most dangerous thing you could ever say in social media. I see it in social bios all the time. Heck, a lot of companies make it a policy that if you're going to be on social media, you must use a disclaimer so that everybody knows whatever you say is not official word from "the" corporation. Just to make sure that you taking a pic of your chicken noodle soup isn't endorsed by Acme Corp.

"All tweets are my own and not a reflection of my employer."

Companies have handled this all wrong. Your employees are a reflection of your company. They are the most important reflections of it. End of story.

Those employee disclaimers hurt more than they help actually because they give people the false sense of freedom with social media speech. If you disclose where you work, you're wearing that name badge 24/7 online. Even if you don't disclose, you're just a LinkedIn search away from being outed.

If you're going to make employees put a disclaimer in their bio, make it this:

> All tweets are my own and a proud reflection of my employer, because we are the brand.

As an example, look what was tweeted recently, one of my favorite examples of a horrible apology:

 Geoffrey Miller
@matingmind

Dear obese PhD applicants: if you didn't have the willpower to stop eating carbs, you won't have the willpower to do a dissertation #truth

6/2/13 12:23 PM

I am *so* glad he added that #truth hashtag just to make sure we all knew he meant what he was tweeting!

When we see a tweet like this, most of us are going to react. But before we do, we usually go and check out just "Who is this jackass?" So let's go together and see just who @matingmind is.

Geoffrey Miller 🔒
@matingmind
Evolutionary Psychology Professor at NYU & U. New Mexico; wrote 'The Mating Mind' and 'Spent'
New York · unm.edu/~psych/faculty..

Well, well. Look who we have here! A psychology professor and part of the PhD selection process at NYU and the University of New Mexico. Makes you wonder about their criteria for applications, doesn't it? And if you'd been considering either of these colleges for study, makes you wonder just what kind of teachers you'd be subjected to.

The Internet reacts—angrily. And he starts the process of Internet Geekalanche Recovery. Picture an angry mob at the top of a mountain like in *Braveheart*, except instead of paint and mud they have ink and toner on their faces.

Step 2: Initial Half-Ass Apology

 Geoffrey Miller
@matingmind

Obviously my previous tweet does not represent the selection policies of any university, or my own selection criteria.

2013-06-02 8:29 PM

 Your Real Name @mazzie   💬 55m
@matingmind you're a coward, a bigot, and a liar.

The word *obviously* really sets the tone for this one! When you are apologizing, I find speaking condescendingly to those upset at you is very effective. Also sarcasm works—as you can see, it's going over smashingly well with the audience.

Step 3: The "Oh Crap, This Is Really Taking Off" Apology

Realizing that he has upset geeks, obese people, and seemingly everyone who isn't a professor at NYU named Miller, he tries again:

Geoffrey Miller
@matingmind

My sincere apologies to all for that idiotic, impulsive, and badly judged tweet. It does not reflect my true views, values, or standards.

2013-06-02 8:21 PM

Wait what? He used the #truth tag!?!?!? Is there no integrity in the #truth tag anymore!?!?!?

I've translated this tweet for you: "My sincere apologies to my boss, who is now reading this thing that they refer to as Tweezer. It does reflect my true views, values, and standards. That's why I used the #truth tag, baby!"

Please listen carefully: When you are on Twitter, you are in public. If you are going to take a stand on a controversial issue, particularly one associated with your workplace, make sure you are ready to stand behind what you're saying. #truth

Step 4: SHUT IT DOWN!!!! SHUT IT DOWN!!!!

@matingmind's tweets are protected.

Only confirmed followers have access to @matingmind's Tweets and complete profile. Click the "Follow" button to send a follow request.

When all else has failed, our higher education friend decides to make his account private, since the #truth hurts. Now one needs to make a request and be accepted to read his crap.

Step 5: Blame Hackers/Virus/Research

This was an unexpected step. This kind of excuse making is usually saved for missent crotch photos. People run to the "I WAS HACKED!

ZOMG!" option, delete quickly, and then look into secluded islands they can relocate to.

Professor Miller takes a new route of the scapegoat in step 5 and decides to claim his original tweet was "for research"! He told the University of New Mexico newsroom that:

> his comment on Twitter was part of a research project. We are looking into the validity of this assertion.[1]

Step 6: Become Known from Here on out as Pulling a Miller

Start a private research lab to discuss the consequences of telling obese people they have no willpower.

Okay, still waiting on step 6, but you get the point.

I truly believe people are forgiving by nature, sometimes a little too forgiving. Even in the face of direct and moral offenses, we want to believe others care enough to be sorry and try to make things right. But we need to be willing to give people the opportunity to forgive us, and more often than not, all we do is make things worse with excuses and finger pointing. Nothing about this would have been different if he'd had a disclaimer in his bio that "all tweets are his own." Aside from a time machine that could have been used to go back to teach our professor how not to be a judgmental jerk, a good apology was his only opportunity. And he failed miserably.

Scott's step-by-step guide on how to apologize in social media:

1. When it hits the fan, don't hide behind the fan. The sooner and more genuine the apology, the more affective it will be.
2. Express remorse without excuses. And if you aren't sorry, then just go with that. Strong opinions breed strong responses.
3. Let your community defend you.
4. Get on with doing good work.

---

[1]Source: http://bit.ly/BadApology (And thanks to my man @supershreve for giving me the heads-up on all of this.)

46

Lack of Tartar Sauce Tact

MISTAKES HAPPEN. Nobody expects a brand or a person to be infallible.[1] Sometimes people come so close to a remedy and then make the whole thing worse. It can be adding a self-serving sentence to an apology post on Facebook. It can be saying "I'm sorry it offended you" versus simply saying "I'm sorry." Or it can be like the experience I had at Red Lobster when I was 13.

For me to recall something that happened 25 years ago that has nothing to do with comic books, *RoboCop,* or the Detroit Lions losing means it has to be pretty impressive—and yet this is a subtle story. My family went out to dinner at Red Lobster, where my siblings and I were getting along not so smashingly, as usual. A waiter walking by accidentally spilled a bright red drink on my older brother. Outside of the immense happiness this caused me at that moment, the waiter appeared sincerely apologetic about staining my brothers $12 dress shirt. He immediately offered to pay for dry cleaning.

So, case closed, right? Mistake happens, apology made, remedy done.

---

[1] Except me, of course.

Except when the server came back with a business card from the restaurant manager, it said on the back of it, "Good for one dress shirt and dress pant dry cleaning <u>ONLY</u>." Just like that, with *only* in all caps and also double underlined.

Even at the innocent age of 13, I wondered if there had been a rash of underground dry cleaning being billed to this Red Lobster location that it needed to have an all-caps stop put to it? Were people going to their buddies and telling them Red Lobster was picking up the dry cleaning tab and collecting their leisure suits?

It didn't make any sense. We weren't in the wrong here, and yet we were treated as though someone was pointing at us with the warning, "Don't try and put one over on us!" And that became the lead of the story whenever it was told over the years.

We create our own company headlines. And the one that my brother had a cold drink spilled all over him would have made the front page of my life, even if it is a common, human mistake thing that happens. Instead, it became about a restaurant that didn't trust its customers. Sure, maybe one in 10,000 people might have gone ahead and had two shirts cleaned, but like most policies where we try to protect ourselves from one person, we end up making it hard for the other 9,999 to do business with us.

Own it, apologize, remedy it, and move on to doing better.

47

Your Community Is an Allen Key

THE AMAZING THING about having a brand community is their devotion and willingness to defend you without being asked. Combine that with the number one demographic you do not want to mess with—breast-feeding moms—and it's like having all of the Scots from *Braveheart* standing on a mountain ready to defend you.

I experienced this firsthand when I posted to the UnMarketing Facebook page[1] a link to a news story about a woman claiming to have been shamed for breast-feeding in a Ottawa, Ontario, at Ikea. Usually, when I see a story from a "real" news station or newspaper site, I assume it has been confirmed and verified, so I didn't think twice about sharing it, knowing full well the outrage that would result in the comments.

But what happened surprised me.

A lot of the comments came out with disbelief: They just couldn't see that happening at an Ikea. People refused to believe a brand/store known for their support of new moms and breast-feeding would act this way. You have to understand that I post brand train wrecks almost daily on that Facebook page, and I've never had this kind of response—questioning the validity of the story—as I did here.

---

[1]You can see the post and comments here: http://bit.ly/UnBreastfeeding

True enough, a few days later, Ikea came out with a statement saying they had reviewed all security footage and interviewed all employees involved and found out that not only had the customer not shopped during the time claimed but when she actually had entered the store and during the duration of her visit, she had been without her baby.

Looking at this, was I in the wrong for sharing the original story? You could argue that I had been, and we will be looking at this a little later in this book. What the community did and how Ikea responded is where the lesson lives.

Between the time Ikea initially apologized and promised an investigation until the time it made the results public, the brand community of customers and supporters virtually circled the wagons and protected the company. The problem with any original story without confirmation going viral is that the investigation and results never catch up to the initial outrage, never reaching the same number of people. This is just human nature. There isn't as much news in a woman not being shamed as there is in the original story.

Also, Ikea's initial apology didn't say much. It was only a sorry and a promise to investigate. No one attempted to placate the customer, make excuses, or take the easy way out. The company stood by its employees and looked into it first, a practice that is rarely seen or talked about.

If Ikea had done the usual public relations move and apologized and offered her some gift cards, attempting to make the whole thing go away, it would never have gone away for the employees who were accused of something they didn't do. Instead, a corporation stood up for the location, something an Allen key can't do.

Ikea's community defended the brand because they just couldn't believe the story was right. Sometimes in social media we are so quick to share these stories that we forget that being right is more important than being first. I shared the story and felt really responsible afterward for giving my community a false story. Everything online moves so fast. We all need to take time to make sure we're sharing good information.

I took the lesson to heart and ever since have been extra cautions when sharing stories. So when I saw the Martin Luther King, Jr., Day special reprinted in the following image, I made sure to check my facts.

I did some research online and checked out the business, Global Village Duluth's Facebook page. The picture was from their annual Martin Luther King Jr. sale and was really happening. Here are the details listed on their page[2]:

> Annual MLK Day BLACK SALE! He showed us that the struggle and lookin' super fly can go hand in hand. We salute him with 25% off everything black, Monday, January 20th. Much more our style than a Columbus Day sale, no?

It was met with the expected negative comments.

I am against using a calendar to dictate when you should blog or what you should blog about. Using world events as topic generators does nothing to establish you as an expert; it just shows you know what day it is.

---

[2] Thanks to Tom Buccheim and Russ Evansen for the heads-up on Twitter.

Since I make my living talking about stories just like this, I was excited to have this shared with me so quickly. It's one of the amazing things about having a community around me to share info. I get the news fast.

The thing is, being first with the news isn't as important as being right. Before sharing the story, I called the store to confirm I wasn't looking at something created in Photoshop to "go viral."

I cannot stress how important checking your facts is. Too many examples in *The Book of Business UnAwesome* were the result of bad information and how quickly it can spread.[3]

It seems the Global Village Store in Duluth, Minnesota, thinks this is a good tie-in. When I phoned them to confirm just now, they excitedly said "Yep! All black items are on sale!"

So, there you go. With confirmation in hand, I sent out the post.

Just. Stop. It.

Show support or respect, or just be quiet. Every occasion isn't a selling occasion. And please, before you share what seems like an unbelievable story, make sure that it doesn't seem that way because it is.

---

[3]http://bit.ly/GlobalVillageSale

48

Return the Brand High Five

I LIVE ON the road, in hotels, and at airports. Whereas some people keep suitcases at the back of their closets, I live out of mine.

So when I read about the Genius Pack on USAToday.com, I was excited to try it out! I trusted the site, and the suitcase was exactly what I'd been looking for. I ordered one that day.

The case arrived quickly and had all the compartments and fancy add-ons I had hoped for (better pockets, phone charger built in, dirty laundry compartment). I was a happy customer and decided to tweet about it.

Scott Stratten ✓
@unmarketing   👤▾ Following

Tryin out my new @GeniusPack suitcase tomorrow. You know you travel a lot when a suitcase excites you.

↩ Reply ↻ Retweet ★ Favorite ••• More

2   **2**
RETWEETS   FAVORITES

4:32 PM - 20 Mar 13

A bunch of my followers jumped in and replied, some of whom were also looking for suitcases. Travel, and anything to make it more comfortable, is a popular topic on Twitter, and the tweet led to a great conversation.

You know who didn't join in though? Genius Pack. The company remained quiet.

When would-be or happy current customers mention your product or service, they are putting up their hands for a high five. It's not to say when we compliment a brand we have to get a reply, but when we make an effort to include the Twitter name, it shows we are including you in the conversation. (I still remember my first reply from a brand, Cirque du Soleil. Love them.) This is an opportunity for engagement that is all too often ignored. As businesses we are quick to reply to angry customers but often leave happy ones hanging.

Genius Pack wasn't listening. Or, if it was, no one was interested in talking with me—or the other would-be customers putting up their hands.

At the time, I didn't think too much about the lack of a reply. I gave the company an opportunity and shared my excitement about the product, but I wasn't sitting around waiting for a response. I took my new suitcase-of-awesomeness, packed it up for the trip, and away we went.

However, by the time I'd reached security at my first airport, I had become frustrated with my new suitcase.

It tipped over. Many times.

It tipped over in line. It tipped over when I let go of it for a moment to take off my jacket. By the time I had finished my trip, the front pocket zipper had broken. (It was far from being over-packed.) I couldn't wait to throw the thing out and use my old suitcase again. The case had been expensive, and instead of making my travel more comfortable, it made it more difficult.

Because I hadn't built a connection to the company, I had no problem voicing my issue publicly.

Scott Stratten ✔ @unmarketing   24 Mar
First trip with @GeniusPack new suitcase. One zipper broken and won't stay standing up. Other than that, it's great.
Details

People replied that they were also looking at this particular suitcase and were glad I saved them the hassle after seeing my original tweet.

When we are endeared to a brand, we seek out private and personal channels to manage resolution. With a brand I know, like, and trust, I will e-mail or contact them privately first, rather than publicly, when I'm unhappy. Because @GeniusPack hasn't followed me, I couldn't send them a private message even if I wanted to.

Unlike the nonreaction to my first tweet, Genius Pack did reply to my second one very quickly.

@unmarketing **Hi Scott, We apologize for the inconvenience, please contact us at info@geniuspack.com & we will work to resolve this with you.**

◄ Reply 🔁 Retweet ⭐ Favorite ••• More

2:48 PM - 24 Mar 13

We went on to e-mail and their CEO was apologetic and very efficient at processing the refund for my purchase—but not before the issue was shared publicly online. I was very impressed by how great they were after the problem, which confused me as to why they had no response before the problem. There weren't hundreds of mentions of the product; actually, there were none other than mine that day.

If you pay attention to your customers only when they are angry, you are going to have only angry customers publicly. You will miss the chance to engage with the happy ones and create brand evangelists. These are the voices that come out of your funnel into the sales cloud. They can either be angry or happy—the choice is yours.

Here are the three steps to create brand endearment.

1. *Listen.* You need to be paying attention to what people are saying about your brand and industry online. There are some great tools out there to help you keep up. It can be as simple as setting up a Google Alert or using keyword search on Twitter. Use a listening

tool such as Expion, Radian6, Vocus, or Trackur. Paying attention is the first step.

2. *Own the good you do.* Value the positive voice. It's too easy to focus only on the negative. You need to make time to thank customers who love what you do. Be proud, and say thank you. (And by "thank you" I don't mean only retweeting positive compliments about yourself. Avoid the humble brag.) I try to do this with people who tweet compliments about my books.

   Don't leave all those high fives hanging. Take time away from fighting fires and seeking out new customers to thank the ones you have. This is where the opportunity for brand endearment begins. Don't value your customers based only on purchases already made. A happy customer is your best marketer. Grow those relationships.

3. *Engage. Social media* is just a fancy term for talking to other people. When you listen and value your customers, you can create content and products that give value back to them. Be a part of the conversation; find out what they like to chat about. Care about what they are looking for. And then be there to have a conversation that matters to them.

When you do these three things, your customers will become endeared to you. You will move their pulse from current customers into ecstatic customers—or at the very least keep them out of the open to competition level.

As customers, we feel like we know an engaged brand, because we do. Brands that connect with their customers online earn a face, a personality, and a reputation for listening. These are the kinds of brands we want to buy from.

49

Stopping the Share

ONCE YOU'VE CREATED great products, services, or content, you don't need to do that much to get people to share it. It's really more about staying out of the way. Here are a few of the worst offenders for getting in the way of sharing.

Flattening Out Word of Mouth

Back in January 2013, BeautyAndFashionTech.com wrote the kind of review of Chi Flat Irons[1] that any product company would be jealous of. They loved the flat iron and gave it a rave review.

That really should be the end of a very short, boring story... it's not.

Rather than thank the site for the love, the parent company of Chi, Farouk Systems, turned around and sued the blog—for copyright infringement.

---

[1]Source: http://bit.ly/ChaChi

Here are just a couple reasons why this is ridiculous.

1. The review was entirely positive, unsolicited by the company, and free. A glowing, unbiased, free review—the gold standard for product companies online. Chi didn't even have to give the site a free flat iron. It's just bad business to try to stop people from saying—to other people and for free!—that they like your product. Companies work long and hard to have a product or service customers love and then to have those customers share their love with the world. Public relations and social media strategist, experts, and managers devote their days to making these things happen.

   Why do anything to get in the way of good reviews? There have been companies and products I previously loved for which I was ready to share stories about until the company decided to send suggested tweets to me, along with the number of times per day they'd like to see them. I once had a phone company let me know I could have a phone to try and then would need to send it back 48 hours later for the honor of writing about it, no payment included. Sending free product to influential people with appropriate targeted platforms can be a great way to let the world know about your company, but doing so with a set of expectations that forces them to a commercial-type promotion isn't what social is all about.

2. What the site did was in no way copyright infringement. As explained on the beauty and fashion tech site, "Trademark infringement is use of a mark in a way that could cause confusion over the ownership of the mark in commerce. Infringement occurs when the use of a trademark is likely to cause consumer confusion as to the source of the item or as to the sponsorship or approval of it. It is not meant to affect free speech."

   If she was manufacturing copycat irons in her basement and marketing Cha Chi flat irons and using the Chi logo, maybe we could talk about copyright. But this just isn't even on the same planet.

So here is what happened. After seeing Beauty and Fashion Tech's response, the public relations manager at Farouk reached out to the company with an apology. Farouk had outsourced the job of monitoring trademark notices to a third party in an effort to stop "Web spam" and never meant for bloggers, especially influential ones who adored their irons, to be targeted.

Really. Suing people is what you've decided to outsource? I am the first person to say you should outsource your weaknesses and/or the things you don't want to do in business to others, but something as important as deciding who to take legal action against? This you may want to keep in house.

The Choice Not to Share

I've never met a blogger who didn't love a share of his or her content. It gives validation and warm fuzzy feelings for all the hard work we do. One of the best pieces of advice I can give to bloggers looking to gain an audience is to go and read blogs, and then comment on and share the ones you love. If you don't have the time to be part of the community, why should anyone else support your blog?

The best way to get your content shared is to write great content. There's no way around this, no matter what anyone tells you. So once you've got the good stuff written, you need to make your site shareable. Sharing buttons are great. But think before you do, please. Make sure the options are appropriate to your content and your readers.

The Sharing Group Hula-Hoop

As the value of social shares has gone up, we've seen more and more groups of people getting together and agreeing to share the sharing. A social circle jerk, where you agree to share all my stuff and I agree to share all your stuff and we all get some shares. The problem is, that isn't what makes things spread. Sharing needs to be based on quality; otherwise, once the content goes past the relationship umbilical cord, it dies.

Mobile

In the fourth quarter of 2013, 64.74 percent of US consumers opened e-mail on mobile devices.[2] That is not a number we can ignore.

---

[2]Source: http://bit.ly/MobileStatsQ4

What difference does it make if your product, service, or content is great if I can't consume it on my phone? When a site takes too long to load or we need to pan and scroll through the pages to read and share, you are losing your readers—no matter how much they would have loved your stuff.

The Bribe

Contests and giveaways have been used as share bribes for a very long time.

"Like our page on Facebook and enter to win."

"Tweet a picture of your meal and receive 10 percent off."

"Pin a photo of your favorite outfit and you can win!"

With the explosion of social media and sharing only being a click away, it's become an epidemic of forced sharing. Legal reasons aside, this can become a very problematic trust issue with your social connections, blog readers, and audience in general.

I choose most of the content I consume through peer recommendations. They act as my content crap filter. If I know Alison has recommended something, it has to be good, because there is no better BS filter than hers. However, if I discovered afterward that she shared an article only because it gave her an entry into a contest, that would make me question future shares.

The FTC recently released new rules around disclosure and contests that require consumers to disclose when they are sharing for the purpose of entering a contest. This was the result of a ruling that found the shoe company Cole Haan was in violation of the FTC after offering one Pinterest user a $1,000 shopping spree if he or she shared the company's products with his or her followers.

The FTC wrote the following to Cole Haan:

The contest rules instructed contestants to create Pinterest boards titled "Wandering Sole." The contest rules further required that a board include five shoe images from Cole Haan's Wandering Sole Pinterest Board as well as five images of the

(continued)

> *(continued)*
> contestants "favorite places to wander." Finally, contestants were instructed to use "#WanderingSole" in each pin description. Cole Haan promised to award a $1,000 shopping spree to the contestant with the most creative entry.[3]

Wow. That is a whole lot of unpaid commercials right there. It comes down to disclosure and keeping content authentic. As long as all of the readers knew the images were being shared so that the pinner could win a prize, it's all good.

This brings up one of the dilemmas those of us in affiliate marketing have been dealing with for years. Is it the contest holder's responsibility to police the sharing, or is it enough for us to have a blanket disclaimer to let people know they need to disclose and then turn a blind eye? Should we be doing a share audit when choosing a winner to make sure all disclosure rules have been followed?

Have I mentioned in no way, shape, or form am I a lawyer? So let's not constitute this, or anything I say, as legal advice.

No Photos, Please

I was at American Apparel shopping for sweatbands and other clothes to film a video for "Bye Bye Bye"[4] when I learned one of the biggest things that stops social sharing. The song, a parody I was writing about unfollowing and unfriending people on social media sites, was set to the musical styling of 'N SYNC, so I needed the kind of gear the store is known for.

I had found some stuff, but I was shopping alone and wanted to get a little bit of help choosing from Alison, so I did what I usually do and went to take a picture of me and some of the options. A salesperson saw me take out my phone and quickly let me know that no pictures were allowed in the store. Why? Because it was "policy." The same company

---

[3] Source: http://bit.ly/ColeHaanPinterest
[4] What? Like you've never done that . . .

that wants me to pin their stuff on Pinterest doesn't want me to take a picture.

Did they really think I was there to grab photos of sweatbands and off the shoulder shirts and send them to a manufacturing ring somewhere? Was I working undercover for Urban Outfitters on a price-matching mission? Look, I understand the no-picture policy in gyms and spots where kids are playing; privacy is important and something we all want to protect. But this was not one of those times.

Shouldn't a store want me tweeting about their products? I don't want to brag, but as a big deal on a fairly irrelevant website that inflates my ego, companies actually try to pay me to share their products online. And here is this store stopping me from even taking a picture.

Pin the Tail on the Brand

Retailers have been falling over themselves to jump on the Pinterest bandwagon. There are certainly ways to leverage it as a brand, especially with a visually pleasing product, with boards and native content that you create yourself. But sometimes you just need to get out of the way. Pinterest is successful because of passion, not profit. The worst thing a brand can do is have pictures of products on its site that aren't pinnable/shareable. (I don't think either of those are real English words by the way.) Having things programmed in Flash is a great way to prevent it from being shared.

If you really want to see how share-friendly your site is, try sharing it as a person on different platforms and using different devices, and see how many barriers you've put up. I've been asked by many marketing executives how to crack the Pinterest code (I'm sure Tom Hanks will play the lead in this movie), and I reply by asking if they've ever tried to pin their own content. The answer is usually no.

50

The Value of a Read

AKA Sensational Headlines Are Evil

SEE WHAT I did there?

If we let it in, the online world can be a very noisy place—but only if we choose it to be. Sensational headlines are used to encourage clicks, but that doesn't mean writing good headlines is inherently bad. We need to be passionate about our content, and the headline is where that starts. Headline writing is an art. I know writers who come up with their headlines first, and then write content around them. Some of us think most creatively in 140 characters; nothing wrong with that.

The best way to encourage quality content isn't necessarily to stop sensational headlines but for us all to stop sharing the bad stuff. As soon as a site gets you once, stop following it. There is too much amazing content out there to allow our time to be focused on the bad.

Upworthy.com is a site known for its headline writing, so I was pleasantly surprised when I read the following quote about what the company feels makes things go viral. You can read the entire post by following the link in your footnote.[1]

---

[1]Source: http://bit.ly/UpWorthyViral

Coming up with catchy, curiosity-inducing headlines wasn't the reason Upworthy had those 87 million visitors. It was because millions of members of the Upworthy community watched the videos we curated and found them important, compelling, and worth sharing with their friends. . . .

"Clickbait"—overselling content with outrageous headlines in order to get people onto a website—is a totally viable (if totally annoying) way to get a bunch of initial views. But it doesn't create viral content. By far the most important factor in getting people to share a post is the actual quality of the content in the eyes of the community. To share, they have to love what they see.

1. Is the content substantive, engaging, and maybe even entertaining?
2. If 1 million people saw it, would the world be a better place?
3. Does the content actually deliver on the promise of the headline?

Compelling content is what the sales cloud is all about. Do people click on lists of the Top Ten Kittens Who LOVE Eating Bacon? Maybe. But that isn't the content that is going to compel people to share great stories about your company. It isn't the kind of content that is going to make you stand out. All that people remember when they see stuff like that online is the kittens. They don't remember where it came from; they don't learn to value your ability to curate online information. They just end up craving bacon. And if you use titles like those or share that kind of content—if you don't deliver and the kitten bacon link takes users to a sale landing page for your accounting business—beware. Nothing is angrier than an online reader who was tricked by kitten bacon.

One of the reasons headlines have become so sensationalized is because of the value we place on the click. The click is king online. The problem is that there are a whole lot of assumptions made in business because of the overvaluing of the click. I accidentally clicked three banner ads just typing this paragraph . . .

I read an incredible article on the subject from Tony Haile on Time.com called "What You Think You Know about the Web Is Wrong" and wanted to share some of the highlights with you.[2]

> The click had some unfortunate side effects. It flooded the web with spam, linkbait, painful design and tricks that treated users like lab rats. Where TV asked for your undivided attention, the web didn't care as long as you went click, click, click.

Why are clicks valuable? I don't know. As a content creator, I want my blog read, shared, commented on, and linked back to. A simple click means nothing to me. It certainly does nothing to enhance the experience or make me stand out to my market.

> It's no longer just your clicks they want, it's your time and attention. Welcome to the Attention Web.

It is impossible to create an experience for anyone in under 15 seconds. "In fact, a stunning 55% spent fewer than 15 seconds actively on a page." Data isn't showing that clicks and reading are the same thing. Topics that are more often clicked are not the same topics that engage the clickers and get read.

> The most clicked on but least deeply engaged-with articles had topics that were more generic. In August, the worst performers included Top, Best, Biggest, Fictional etc while in January the worst performers included Hairstyles, Positions, Nude and, for some reason, Virginia. That's data for you.

> A widespread assumption is that the more content is liked or shared, the more engaging it must be, the more willing people are to devote their attention to it. However, the data doesn't back that up. We looked at 10,000 socially-shared articles and found that there is no relationship whatsoever between the amount a piece of content is shared and the amount of attention an average reader will give that content.

---

[2]http://time.com/12933/what-you-think-you-know-about-the-web-is-wrong/

That may be the most important thing you ever read about social. Sharing does not necessarily mean a reader has given attention. So, if you are creating content and evaluating how successful it has been for you, focusing only on shares won't give you a full picture. And if you create content based on what gets shared the most, you aren't doing yourself any favors. As businesses, we need our content consumed—not just clicked on, not just shared. If we believe social is a tool for being noticed in the sales cloud, we need our market's attention. The only way to do that is with compelling, worth-more-than-15-seconds-of-your-time content. Otherwise, you can take the shares and likes you've been counting and consider them a waste of time.

51

Avoid the Cleanse

How to Keep Your Subscribers

Recognized, Relevance, Relationship

In *UnMarketing*, we spoke about e-mail and how important[1] your
mailing list is, even in today's social media–focused online world.
E-mail is still valuable and targeted and is the best way to reach an
audience who has opted in for your content. Whether or not our
kids will use e-mail remains to be seen, but for now I would rather
have a subscriber list than a following. When people subscribe to your
newsletter, they are putting their hand up, asking to stay in touch
with you. This is a huge opportunity to send useful information and be
helpful—remember in UnSelling, we don't use our newsletters only
to push discounts. No one signs up for your newsletter for you; they
sign up for themselves.

That said, my own inbox can be a very busy place.

I've been cleansing for the past week. Not one of *those* cleanses
that your friends post about on Facebook that makes you cringe, but an
inbox cleanse. I'm trying to clear my inbox and stay on top of it. I was

---

[1] I would argue that e-mail is the most valuable customer digital asset.

at 1,800+ e-mails that needed my attention a few days ago and am now down to 140. One of the things I've been doing is unsubscribing from almost every newsletter I've been on. Only a select few have survived from the dozens, if not 100+ I was on. Why did they stay?

Recognized, relevance, relationship.

I *recognized* the sender and remember signing up in the first place.

The content is *relevant* to me, not just relevant to the sender, like a sales pitch.

I feel a connection to the brand, like a *relationship*.

Really, there are three classifications of e-mail that we all receive:

1. Spam/trash/not reading
2. Will read later
3. Must read/react

Stay out of the first two categories, because *will read later* is Latin for "not reading later; see it three months from now, feel guilty, delete, and pretend I never got it."

Here are some tips to get yours into the must read category:

- Get them in the door in the first place. Having a box on your website that says "Sign up for our free newsletter" is not enticing. Besides, since when was the free part unique? Are there a rash of crappy paid newsletters that are taking over the nation that I didn't know about? How about "Sign up for product updates and exclusive announcements" if you're a product business? Or something like "Sign up for weekly tips on how to save your business money" if you're a service business?
- When I do sign up, send me a welcome e-mail, not a confirmation e-mail. There is a big difference. A confirmation e-mail is, "You've been added to the BoringAsPaint newsletter. 8490283HJF-94," or even better, "You've been added. Here's the info you just entered into the form." Someone signing up for your newsletter/blog update list is raising a hand for a brand high five, and we're leaving most of them hanging. Do you know how stupid people feel when they're left hanging for a high five? It's almost as embarrassing as tweeting about a juice cleanse. Welcome them. Talk to them. Start a conversation.

When you sign up for my newsletter, my welcome e-mail says:

> Hi there,
>   Thanks for signing up to the Un-Marketing newsletter. I know how an inbox can get crowded, and I appreciate you allowing my newsletter to get through the clutter.
>   May I ask what line of business you're in? It helps me tailor the newsletter to you even better.

Really, it does; go see for yourself on UnMarketing.com and you'll get e-mailed only when I have something awesome to say for your business (see what I did there?).

You know what that reply e-mail does for me? It creates a connection with the reader and automatically sets the tone for future e-mails. Most don't reply, and of the ones who do, half are replying to say they like the fact that I asked! For the ones that do, I read them. I get them right to my phone, and I reply to a lot of them. I used to have them go to my assistant, but then I realized that missed the point of the reason I was asking it in the first place: I wanted to know, and even though my initial reply is automated, I always read their replies and respond personally.

Not only does this create a connection but I've had awesome conversations with people because of it and it's led to book sales and speaking gigs. When researching speakers about "engagement" for a conference coming up, the booker subscribed to a few newsletters of potential keynotes. Guess who the only one was who actually engaged with her? I'm looking forward to keynoting that conference. For those of you saying, "Whoa, cowboy! We can't handle that amount of e-mail replies!" Relax. The three subscribers you're getting a week won't overload the server with responses. Even a big brand shouldn't have a lot of issues. I had a newsletter in a different industry with more than 350,000 subscribers, thousands coming in a day. Most people don't reply; they just like the fact you asked.

When you connect with your readers, your brand is no longer a brand, but a conversation they've had. When your name pops into their inbox again, they recognize you. Forget the "best time of day to send e-mail"; if they don't recognize you, it doesn't matter what time it is when their newsletter arrives.

Every touch point with a customer is an opportunity to move the pulse. That includes newsletter sign-ups and even confirmation e-mails. Just because something is automated in e-mail, doesn't mean it can't be fun and reflect your company. Here is a great example of a fun confirmation e-mail from JulieHarrison.ca. You can check her out by using the link in your footnote.[2]

Your Fluevogs can't wait to meet you . . .
We wanted to let you know about a change to the status of your Fluevog order, placed on 2012-Jul-22.
Your order is now complete!

1. Your order was carefully taken from our Dot Matrix and passed to our Fluevogian Elves, who started searching for your exact item(s).
2. Our well-trained packing specialist gathered everything needed to do the best packing job he could, especially for you. Only when completely satisfied with his deliverable, he sent word to the FluevogFleet using incensed smoke signals.
3. We welcomed the Fleet which always consists of three solar-powered FluevogVans—one for security, one for your package, and one for refreshments and supplies. We briefly chatted about what great taste you have and how good looking you are, but then they were off and on their way to make the final delivery.

(Please note: We occasionally outsource transportation to our well-trusted partners, as demand continues to increase and running multiple Three Van Fleets gets expensive for a small, powerful shoe company.)

---

[2]http://bit.ly/Fluevogs

How great is that? And what the heck is a Fluevog? Because now I want some! This is such a great example of a company using a pulse point to make a customer experience that much better. This is the kind of experience that is shared and talked about. Fluevog didn't set out to be on her blog, or mine, or for you to be reading about the company here. The Fluevog team just had a little fun and chose to make a usually boring confirmation e-mail something worth smiling about.

My favorite place to buy T-shirts and help causes,[3] Sevenly.org, sends a confirmation that includes the line below:

Thanks Scott Stratten! **Your middle name should be 'generous'**

- Make it personal. I can't stand automation; that's no secret. When it comes to newsletters, when I say *automation*, I mean sending out blog posts and the copy that goes with it, the feed-looking notification that a new post is up or even the cut-off intro to the post. I write a custom e-mail to my list when a new blog post is up, just for them. It's short and fun, and I love writing them.
- Respect your readers. I've said this many times in books and talks: E-mail your list only when you have something to say that's useful for them, not because you "should" send something weekly. I rarely blog, but when I do, people open the e-mail about it because if my lazy ass wrote something, it has to be good. I promise you, no one will get to Wednesday and not see your newsletter and miss you if the only thing you ever send out are discounts. And I double promise you that no one will read an amazing newsletter from you and say it would have been better if only it had arrived Tuesday at 11 AM.

Every month a new "study" comes out to say when the best time is to send e-mail out to your list/subscribers/mother.

One study said between 12 AM and 3 AM.[4] Another said between 8 AM and 10 AM and between 3 PM and 4 PM.[5] Or for the early crowd, one study recommended from 6 AM to 7 AM.[6]

---

[3]Seriously, I have 57 Sevenly T-shirts. And you should have some, too.
[4]Source: http://bit.ly/SendEmailNow
[5]Source: http://bit.ly/SendEmailNow2
[6]Source: http://bit.ly/SendEmailNow3

If I looked hard enough, I could probably find studies that cover every hour of every day.

The best time to never send e-mail is when someone else told you to. Do your homework. The only important data out there is what your own list does.

I've been doing e-mail marketing since the old days when you sent an e-mail and everyone received it. Remember that? When the e-mail alert went off, you got excited!

The biggest mistake with looking at when to send to your list is we think that's our issue. We think we're getting low open rates because we sent a newsletter at 11 AM EST on a Wednesday instead of 5 AM PST on a Thursday.

The Best Way to Get Your E-Mail Opened Is to Write Content Worthy of Being Opened

When notification of your new blog post or newsletter arrives to your subscribers, do they react with apathy or excitement?

If your subject line is "ABC Chiropractor Newsletter January Edition," no one is going to care what time you send it out. No one puts aside their game of Flappy Bird to read that headline.

People first have to recognize your "From:" as a brand they want to read, then the subject, then the content itself. Fix those things first, and then test, test, test. But don't test with different e-mails over a few weeks; test the same one. Create one variable—delivery time—and split test them with your e-mail service if they allow it.

Stop changing how you market your business because of a headline; that's why you read best-selling books like *UnSelling*. :) The only important case study is the one you're currently running for your business.

52

Should You Trade in Trade Shows?

"SCOTT, IN THE world of social media, are trade shows even important anymore?"

I get asked this all the time—mostly because I keynote a ton of events with trade shows and attend a few myself. The answer is yes. Trade shows aren't that different from social media in that they are a tool, an opportunity to meet and connect with your market. The value of a trade show can't be measured in sales alone, but should also factor in the face-to-face contact you get with individuals who are interested in learning more about your product or service. Unlike in social media, which is made up of selfish platforms about me,[1] the attendees at a trade show are there to learn more about buying from you.

1. Trade shows are like social media because being successful at both starts with treating people like people, not prospects—a key concept of *UnSelling* that cannot be overstated. Even on a trade show floor, where people are walking the aisles expecting to be sold to, the most successful product brands will always remember that it

---

[1]Not *me*, but you or us. You know what I mean.

can't be buy or good-bye. As I wrote in *UnMarketing*, the best trade show salespeople practice what I call pull and stay—connecting, collecting prospective customer information, and then staying in front of them with useful content.

2. Trade shows are like social media because being successful at both is a whole lot easier with a great product or service. On trade show floors, having quality product cannot be faked. People try—with swag that people will take, never remembering where they got it. Booths can fight to outflash one another, but nothing beats a good product people need. Trade show swag is the real-life version of a keyword-rich tweet. Sure, it may get some eyes on you, but it won't take people long to see there's nothing there worth their time.

3. Trade shows are like social media because no one likes a mooch. The worst people at trade shows by far are the suitcasers. I'd take any aggressive salesperson or hungover marketer sleeping in a booth over these guys. Without paying for a booth, they wander the aisles pushing products to vendors—vendors who have spent hard-earned money and a ton of time getting ready for the show, only to be distracted by these wanderers! In social, they could be compared to accounts that sell before giving to the community. We need to give first, before we take.

4. Trade shows are not like social media because you need to wear pants to trade shows. One of the hot topics about trade shows today, and related to the clothes wearing situation we just touched on, is booths hiring "booth babes" and whether in today's world that is still an acceptable, or successful, practice. Booth babes are defined as women hired only for looks; the term does not apply to knowledgeable salespeople who also happen to be attractive.

I read a great article on the subject by Spencer Chen on Tech Crunch.[2]

He did a split test at a trade show, where one of their booths used booth babes and the other didn't. They found that the booth without the babes did better.

> The booth that was staffed with the booth babes generated
> a third of the foot traffic (as measured by conversations

---

[2]http://bit.ly/BoothBabes

or demos with our reps) and less than half the leads (as measured by a badge swipe or a completed contact form) while the other team had a consistently packed booth that ultimately generated over 550 leads, over triple from the previous year.

From the split test, he concluded that the booth babes were intimidating and generally not as hardworking as other booth attendants and that the leads they generated were of low quality, if anyone would speak to them at all. Some attendants and media feel strongly that writers are refusing to write about booths that staff them.[3] Using booth babes is a lot like using swag, especially swag unrelated to your product. At the end of a show, if the attendees remember your incredible giveaway iPad case or walking stick but can't remember where they got it, you've just wasted a whole lot of money. Both are the sensational headline equivalent at a trade show. The babes at the front may be memorable; they may turn some heads and even get a few extra eyes on your booth. But it the eyes remember the person and not the product—and if they don't come into the booth and just keep walking—you've done more damage than good.

Trade shows are a tool and an opportunity to spread the word about your brand, meet new and potential customers, and connect with your peers. There isn't a bigger social media fanboy than me, but nothing online beats face to face. Decide what you want to get from a trade show and make it happen. And remember to think outside the funnel and measure your successes in UnSelling terms, not sales numbers.

---

[3]Source: http://bit.ly/MoreBoothBabes

53

What Really Matters in Speaking

IN A PREVIOUS life, I spoke in human resources circles about work-life balance. Some would say I was a motivational speaker.[1] While being the Canadian Tony Robbins, I was giving a keynote in Baltimore to 200 nurses, and I killed it. Everything came together, and I had the right mix of content, charisma, and timing. I got my first ever standing ovation. It was unreal.

As I walked off the stage, the next speaker came up to me. I expected a high five or congratulations on my talk, but that's not what she had in mind. While I was still receiving the standing ovation, she let me know that her talk was about colors that you wear and how my choice of an all black outfit had been a mistake, because it didn't complement me. Can you read that entire story back again to yourself and picture it? I failed to mention that this "color expert" was wearing a flower print muumuu at the time, which I believe covered every color in the spectrum. That's when I realized it: It didn't matter. It didn't even faze me. The only thing that matters in speaking is that your content resonates with the audience and is delivered in a way that allows them to absorb it.

---

[1] Ya, I know, I just ooze positivity and motivation.

You can have content without delivery, and you can have good delivery without content. But when you combine them both, you've done your job.

Standing ovations don't even matter. Did the audience walk out of your talk better than they were when they walked in? Is the person who hired you ecstatic about that choice? If you just filled the time, that's simply not good enough.

You don't have to be me, flailing around, yelling; you just need to speak with conviction about something you know about and have the content to back it up. The only question with any merit afterward is, If they had to do it again, would the people who hired you do it again? I've read ridiculous articles on speaker association websites[2] that talk about stage anchoring: the art of standing at different spots on the stage depending on whether your message is negative or positive. I've been asked, I mean told, to wear a tie. And I've seen speakers ask people to stand up and stretch at the end of their talk and call it a standing ovation.

None of it matters. You're not supposed to be a speaker; you're supposed to be an expert who can speak. I make my living doing this, not only because I know how to talk, but because I know the industry I talk about. I make knowing about it a full-time job.

---

[2] Are there any other kind?

54

What Really Matters in Podcasting

DIVING INTO THE world of podcasting with the UnPodcast[1] came with a lot of "rules" that seemingly changed depending on whom we talked to. We heard your show intro needed to be 3 percent of the length of the show and that episodes should be only 30 minutes, only 45 minutes, only an hour. You shouldn't have two hosts. Your topic needed to be niche. You should always have guests to keep the topics fresh. And always, always plan ahead.

So we took all the advice and did what we usually do: followed none of it—because it came from people we didn't know and hadn't asked. We listened to Cliff Ravenscraft, the Podcast Answer Man.[2] We listened to shows we liked. And then went with what was most "us": shows with no fixed length, no guests, and no plan. We would talk about what we were interested in for as long as we found it interesting and hoped others would as well.

There were so many rules that it became paralyzing for anyone to start a new one, and most of it didn't matter. At the time of writing

---

[1] You can watch and listen at unpodcast.com
[2] Check out Cliff's site for more info at podcastanswerman.com

this, we just surpassed 150,000 downloads, and yet our first ever piece of feedback from episode 1 was:

 Glenn Hansen · 8 months ago
I love podcasts, but 56 minutes? Correct, I shouldn't judge before I listen to this one. But 56 minutes?
1 ∧ | ∨ · Reply · Share ›

He hadn't even listened to it yet! It's enough to make most people question what they're doing. But we've made it into a running joke instead, artificially finishing each episode at 15 minutes in case people want off the podcast train. We had someone comment that he loved the almost-hour-long episodes but could we maybe cut them into three 20-minute episodes. I'm not sure you could picture the look on my face when I first read that or even now as I'm writing about it, but it's quite epic. It's called a pause button.

When you're making content, if you're true to yourself, the content comes out most naturally. We've never had more fun than we do making the podcast and its sister podcast, the Vegas30,[3] and that comes out in each episode. That's the biggest piece of feedback we get: that it sounds like we love doing them, which makes them fun to listen to. I've been in content marketing for 20 years, and there's never been a more passionate audience than a podcast one—or a more judgmental one.

Podcasting has a very low barrier to entry, which we love. It means anyone can start one with a few simple tools. Some of the most popular are grassroots, do-it-yourself formats. You can hire people to help with sound recording and editing; you can have your podcast filmed like we do and shoot it at a studio. You can bring in guests or hire dancers for all we care. But you can't outsource passion, knowledge, and fun. People will forgive technical issues, but they won't stick around for boring. Part of putting your work out there is feedback, but make sure you don't let the feedback keep you from remembering why you started.

If you're going to do it, do it well, do it right, and, of course, make sure every episode is 56 minutes. :)

---

[3]Go to Vegas30.com for episodes.

55

What Really Matters in Blogging

As I TRAVEL the world speaking about blogging and UnSelling, I hear a lot about work and time—mostly about how there is too much work and not enough time.

"Sure, Scott, we understand how blogging has worked for you. But we just don't have enough time!"

"I know you said that if you believe business is built on relationships, you should make building them your business . . . but isn't that an awful lot of work?"

"I'd love to blog/use Twitter/use Facebook/reply to customers, Scott. I just don't have enough time!"

We make time for the things we find valuable. You make time to answer the phone, and I'm sure you always have enough time to collect payment from your customers and clients. You're making time to read this book.

One of the parts of social media that can take up the most time is a blog. You need to write it, share it, and be around to reply to comments. I am tired already just thinking about it.

A blog is also one of the most valuable tools for businesses. Unlike Facebook or Twitter, where brands spend a ton of time collecting likes, a blog belongs to you. You own the content and control the rules. You also have some space to position yourself as an expert, unlike the quick format of social sites. A blog allows you to build community: Readers become commenters, and commenters add to the conversation and talk to you and to one another.

Even with all these factors that make blogging an opportunity for brands, it seems to be the number one thing people question the value of. Following are some of my favorite reasons they give for why.

1. No Return on Investment (ROI)

How do you measure the value of sharing your knowledge online, engaging with customers, and fostering a community based around your product or service?

Here is a list of the business-related returns Alison gained from writing her business blog for Nummies Bras.

- Conversations with customers (including answering questions, solving problems, and hearing about how awesome we were)
- Conversations with prospective customers (about pregnancy, breast-feeding, and parenting)
- Market research (questions and feedback from customers and prospective customers)
- Meeting of the minds (support and debate from others in my industry)
- Increased brand awareness (blog shared in social media and by traditional media channels online)
- Fostering of community around product (conversations and connections between customers)
- Marketing (blog shares that reached people who were not previously aware of the brand)

2. Industry Regulations

Some of the very best social media accounts and blogs come from industries you wouldn't think could be awesome. Police departments, which could not face more issues of confidentiality and regulation, have some of our favorite accounts, which are both personal and professional, while maintaining regulations and providing a human face to their organizations. Products as seemingly commonplace as tractors and industrial fans wow us with their use of blogs to connect and market their lines. Your industry not seeming open to blogging just means there is more room for you to shine. Start with being helpful to your clients and go from there.

3. No Time

You are making time to read this. We make time for the things we see value in. The same is true for blogging and social media. They can take up as little or as much time as you decide.

Or as Julie Cole, cofounder of Mabel's Labels, blogger and mother to six, replied once to an audience member asking her about time, "Don't tell me you have no time."

4. Business-to-Business (B2B)

There is just as much potential value in B2B business blogging as there is for business-to-consumer (B2C) blogging. We are all people, and the importance of connecting with others and positioning yourself as an expert in your field is no different when businesses are your potential clients. Plus, in B2B your target audience tends to be smaller and easier to define, which makes a blog even easier to create, share, and grow.

5. I Don't Have Anything to Say

If you don't have anything to say about your industry, product, or service, then why should customers be interested in exchanging their hard-earned currency for your work? Start with the pain points and needs of your potential customer and how your business answers those for them. It doesn't need to be funny, epic, or beautiful. It just needs to be helpful. You are running a business, and your blog should be thought of as a product you are providing. It's not a test or someplace to just throw up things because it's Tuesday and someone told you always to blog that day. Value your would-be customers' time.

6. I'm Scared of Negative Comments and Reactions

When you put yourself and your business out there online, negativity can come your way.

As an entrepreneur I need to tell you that a few negative blog comments will not be the toughest thing you need to be able to stomach. You are going to need thick skin. There will be rejections, long hours, little pay, sleep deprivation, and then more rejections. This whole business thing is not easy, and I suggest if you are crippled with fear by the possibility of negativity that this may not be the game for you.

Your business blog is a representation of your brand and one of the best ways to position yourself as an expert and/or go-to product. It needs to be good and helpful. This is not a place to test out your writing style or play around with your message. Your business blog isn't a training bra; it's the real thing, and you need to treat it that way. Use the same care when you create content as you do when you create a new product. Make it good, and then don't be too scared to share it with the world.

56

Company-Created Community

UNSELLING IS ABOUT creating and facilitating a community based around your product. So you've managed to win the funnel vision game, and someone has chosen you as her product or service of choice. You've managed not to mess it up during the sale, and you have a happy customer. Congratulations, you used to be done. But not with us. With *UnSelling*, your work is just beginning.

The most successful brands have a community of fans around them. Companies such as Apple, Disney, Lululemon, and Whole Foods have leagues of people who feel connected to other customers by the shared experience that an iPhone or yoga pants bring. So how do the greats do it?

1. *They create opportunities for fans to connect and talk to one another, not to the brand.* A blog is the perfect place to start with this for your business. The wonderful thing about a blog—well, one of the wonderful things—is the way a post comes to life in the comments. Here, readers add their opinions and can talk to one another about the topic on your site. You own the conversation here; you can protect commenters from spam and trolls, fan the fires, and actually own the content. And when people start writing their own blogs

215

about your products, that's the first way to see your community growing.

Now we can also learn from the great what not to do, as Lululemon taught us when it went after some huge fans for reselling pants online. The company has a very strict resell policy, one I am sure is in line with health issues around a product hippies do a lot of sweating in. However, some of the people they went after and shut out of the website were megafans who were running fan sites and everything! One of the bloggers had founded the site LuluMen and spent more than $10,000 personally on product from the company. A good customer and an ambassador is maybe not who you should be blocking from your site. Lululemon did eventually apologize to him but stood behind the policy, saying it was to protect customers from counterfeit and damaged goods.[1]

2. *Share things your customers like—and I don't mean sales or your product.* One of the best examples of this and how it creates community is the Whole Foods Pinterest page.[2] The company has more than 50 boards on the site, including those for recipes and food. But that's not where the pinning stops! Whole Foods shares kitchens on the board "Super HOT Kitchens," gadgets and tech on the "Go, Go Gadget" board, staff's favorite books, vacations, and much, much more. Fans love the page. It shows the store is about more than just what you take through the checkout line. And through the page, Pinterest users can connect with one another. This goes for all social media platforms. When I was getting started, I connected more on Twitter talking about poker and music than I ever did talking about marketing.

3. *Be a help.* Community is about support and helping one another out. Companies that do community creation right give back. We can create opportunities for fans to get together and support one another or the causes we care about. And I do not mean some tiny percentage of sales going to charity. I mean real giving. The past two Christmases, on the UnMarketing Facebook page, I started a thread buying items off people's Amazon wish lists. The best part about the thread was that people started jumping in and buying for one another: The page created the opportunity.

[1]Source: http://bit.ly/LuluBan
[2]www.pinterest.com/wholefoods/

57

Up the Customer Creek

IN THE WORLD of social media, things move fast. Tweets have a shelf-life of no more than a few moments, and videos popular today are quickly replaced by the next big thing tomorrow. Immediacy is a critical component for companies managing online conversations about brands. As customers we want and expect things quickly—our replies, our products, and our Amazon orders.

The same is true in business, especially when you work in marketing and technology. The focus is always on new start-ups and Kickstarter campaigns. We jump ahead to what's next before we ever fix what's now. Patience seems to be going the way of the CD and the newspaper, a relic we tell our kids we used to have.

That's why when I heard the story of Forty Creek Whisky I knew it was special. John Hall was a winemaker who grew up in Windsor, Ontario, Canada. When he was a kid, there were two possibilities for future jobs: working in the automotive industry or working at the Hiram Walker Distillery. Cars weren't his thing, but after graduating with a degree in food chemistry, he was turned down by the distillery. He decided to follow his passion and went to work for a winery in the Niagara region, where he stayed, moving up the ladder until 1992, when he left to start his own company. He found a small distillery in

Grimsby, Ontario, purchased the property, and followed his dream of making his own brand of Canadian Whisky.

Now, unlike many of today's products, whisky takes time and lots of it. The whiskey he started creating in 1992 would not be ready for market until 10 years later. Imagine investing that much time and effort into a product. John knew he could create something amazing, and he had the forethought and the dedication to make that happen.

In 1992, the wine and spirit industry was going through a major rationalization. Small companies were being bought up by huge multinationals. Although as iconic as maple syrup or hockey, Canadian whisky was being lost in the mix. There were no other products on the market at that time that took pride in the name, and John knew he could change that. He wanted to bring heritage and craftsmanship back to Canadian whisky.

Ten years passed. John ran a winery on the premises in the meantime to keep funding the dream. The wine products themselves were very successful, but the goal remained to focus 100 percent on whisky making. The results were outstanding. There isn't a whisky competition out there that Forty Creek hasn't won a gold medal in. Following his winemaking roots, John added tasting notes to the bottle labels, something no other whisky had. He wanted to show people that his product was something special.

When the first bottles of Forty Creek hit shelves, they were not a success. Even with awards and quality on their side, customers just weren't buying. John decided this was unacceptable. He went on the road, visiting LCBO[1] locations and conducting tastings and staff training seminars. He stood for hours in stores, sharing his story and endearing store staff to the brand. Even today, when Forty Creek asks customers how they found out about the product, more often than not it is from an LCBO staff recommendation. John's dedication and commitment to his story and building relationships worked, and news of his product spread.

Now, a 10-year-old product in waiting may seem patient to us, but in the world of whisky, Forty Creek is still in its infancy. Some of its

---

[1]Liquor Control Board of Ontario, the world's largest single purchasers of alcoholic beverage products. These are a chain of retails stores where us Ontarians can buy wine and other alcoholic beverages.

competitors have been around since prohibition days and had loyal customer bases not willing to try something new. But John kept at it. He knew that with a product as high quality as his, with a rich heritage and authentic story, that if he could just get people to try it, they would switch. And switch they have. New customers consider finding the brand a badge of pride and share it with their friends.

Forty Creek has embraced social media. The company uses it to connect with fans online and amplify John's voice worldwide. Each year, Forty Creek produces a limited special edition run and holds an event called Whisky Weekend.[2] Last year, only 9,000 bottles of a special reserve called Heart of Gold was the star. Customers could purchase the numbered bottles ahead of time under one condition: They had to make the trip to Grimsby to pick up their bottle. Thousands of people showed up for the weekend. This year will mark the eighth Whisky Weekend, and some people have all seven bottles in their collections. Customers return for the same number each year, some with special significance, like a police badge number or the last year the Maple Leafs won the Stanley Cup.[3]

Social media has added to the event, because pictures and stories make it possible to share the experience with a much broader audience. Fans will tweet questions to John about whisky making, and the community of fans who come together for the weekend can use it to stay in touch after and connect before. Forty Creek customers feel a part of the brand, and they want it to succeed.

In 1992, Forty Creek was a small start-up company in an industry ruled by global brands. They had no marketing budget for traditional media, just John and his passion and will to work until people took notice. The quality of the product stood strong, and as word spread, customers started doing John's job for him so he could focus on what he does best: making Canadian whisky people love.

---

[2]http://fortycreekwhisky.com/Whisky_weekend.html
[3]*cough* 1967.

58

Passive versus Active Exposure

REMEMBER BACK IN Chapter 21 when I told you about the York Police department's Twitter account and how much we adore them? The police use Twitter to reply to community concerns and questions and share relevant information about safety and law enforcement. They use Twitter to be part of their community, because their community is using Twitter. They do the work of engagement and are present online, as they are on Toronto streets.

For them, Twitter isn't a campaign. It isn't a way to show off their good work. Their exposure online is passive; they do what they do, and the community speaks for them. I sure do.

The key to social according to *UnSelling* is to work toward passive versus active exposure. This means we want to create experiences worth sharing, rather than sharing our experiences for ourselves. Active exposure is the push, where businesses and organizations go on Twitter and other platforms and send out their messages using social media like a modern-day, 24-hour-a-day/seven-day-a-week press release where they control the message. Active exposure can also mean trying to control the conversation through sponsored hashtags and Twitter events. Remember the good old days when you could craft a marketing campaign and send it out, controlling the images people would see of, and about, your brand? Well, on social media that kind of active exposure just doesn't work.

As a counterpoint to the social success of the Toronto and other police forces discussed before, let's look at a campaign from the New York City Police Department. The NYPD decided to create its own hashtag and asked the Twitter community to take photos with their police department members and share them. The hashtag #myNYPD may have seemed harmless enough, but when you try to force the active share, things can really backfire.

The NYPD tweeted:

> Do you have a photo w/ a member of the NYPD? Tweet us
> & tag it #myNYPD. It may be featured on our Facebook.

And as explained on reuters.com,[1] things didn't go according to plan.

Twitter decided to give the account exactly what they asked for: photos of individuals with the police department. However, these images were often violent and rarely positive, including pictures of police brutality, pepper spray use, and violent arrests. And all were neatly posted with a hashtag included for easy search.

The initial post was done on a Tuesday, and "by Wednesday morning, the #mynypd hashtag had been tweeted more than 94,000 times. By afternoon, the viral campaign had spread across the country, sparking similarly critical images and tweets around hashtags aimed at police departments in Miami, Detroit, Los Angeles, Oakland and Chicago."

The images shared attached to the hashtag could not be ignored. They were highly emotive, upsetting, and certainly worth a social share. The campaign was started with the best of intentions, but you simply cannot force people online to share your messages. They want to share their own.

Another great example of the value of passive exposure comes to us from Ikea, one of the most recognized and popular brands out there. We spoke about marketing to women when we discussed motivation and pulse—and how taking that stand can backfire the way it did for Bic Pens. In Canada, according to research foundation

---

[1]Source: http://bit.ly/NYPDHashtag

Marketel, "women buy half of all cars, make 93% of over-the-counter pharmaceutical decisions and are responsible for 80% of home improvement projects." Marketel names Ikea as women's top 9 brand (others included Costco and Apple), because "IKEA is a playground for women 'delivering affordable, stylish living and unleashing the designer inside me... all on a budget' gushed one respondent."[2]

With this information, it might seem in a brand's best interest to actively market to women—and yet this kind of active exposure, more often than not, offends the very people they are trying to reach.

Ikea, on the other hand, sends a much more passive message. It doesn't launch shopping carts with tiny handles so as not to harm women's dainty arms;[3] it simply creates environments where shoppers' needs are met, including providing child-friendly shopping spaces, affordable prices, and stylish products. No all-caps go-women-go hashtags required. This marketing has been so effective that the community of fans will even come out in support of the brand, as we saw in Chapter 47, when it was accused of non–family-friendly treatment of a customer.

Passive exposure is about creating content that's reactionary. You do the work or make the product. You provide the customer service and put those amazing frontline workers in place. And those experiences create a reaction, a reaction where people want to tell everyone they know about you. We don't often think about our products and service as content, but in terms of online marketing, that's exactly what it is. Whether a great experience at a theme park, a car, or a meeting with a dentist, your job as a business is to start thinking about the things you do as experiences and as content to be shared. Stop pushing out what you want people to say, stop forcing hashtags for contests, and focus on creating things worthy of reaction.

---

[2] Source: http://bit.ly/BrandsWomenLove
[3] Please see the sarcasm.

59

The Inner Social Circle

THE BOMBARDMENT OF social media with advertisements and brand accounts has led more and more people into the inner social circle. This is the real key to why push messaging in social media will no longer work going forward. This is why continuing to focus on the funnel and active exposure in sales needs to stop and *UnSelling* needs to start happening.

When Facebook bought WhatsApp, a personal real-time messaging network allowing millions of people around the world to stay connected with their friends and family, for a gazillion dollars ($19 billion, to be exact), the world took notice. Mark Zuckerberg himself explained the purchase on the Facebook blog: "WhatsApp is on a path to connect 1 billion people. The services that reach that milestone are all incredibly valuable."[1]

Facebook sees us common folk avoiding ads at every turn and valuing our privacy—that's why the world's leading social network starts investing in a private messaging company. Collecting our search data is what it does, packaging it to advertisers. Facebook sees in all this data

---

[1] Source: http://bit.ly/WhatsAppPurchase

that we don't go on Facebook to talk to brands; we want to talk to our friends and Facebook and other companies in the connection business know it.

Content and experiences will always be shared, but more and more they will be shared privately. When social media first took off, the growth was organic and we were all just there to talk. Ah, the good ole days ... Then brands started inviting themselves to the conversations, not only to reply to customer service questions and complaints, but to use the forum and push out their messages—and a problem began. Companies have had years to see passive conversations about their brands and competition, but that wasn't enough. They needed to try to control the conversations, and people have pushed back.

Jan Koum, WhatsApp cofounder and chief executive officer (CEO), said, "WhatsApp's extremely high user engagement and rapid growth are driven by the simple, powerful and instantaneous messaging capabilities we provide."[2]

He keeps a note on his desk that says:

No Ads

No Games

No Gimmicks

Those three lines are a breath of fresh air in a social world that has become about sponsored posts, push messages from games, and click trickery. Now, this isn't to say that these kinds of apps, once bought, won't bow to the same pressures that have affected Twitter and Facebook. You need to know that Mr. Zuckerberg didn't spend all that money not wanting a return on his investment. The difference we may see is that the value of social sites, the users, are changing as the population changes—and expectations are changing with them.

The next generation of consumers, teens, are taking great care to control their privacy, much more than twentysomethings have. According to Mashable Business, "Only 11% of 14- to 18-year-olds share 'a lot about themselves online,' down from 18% a year ago, and compared with 17% of 19- to 24-year-olds and 27% of 25- to 34-year-olds, the youth-focused consumer insights group found in a

[2]Source: http://bit.ly/WhatsAppFor19B

survey of 1,300 people. About 60% of that youngest group said they 'don't like things that last forever online,' compared with 53% or less among 19- to 34-year-olds."[3]

That is a pretty dramatic decrease in sharing. And as a parent of a teen and soon-to-be teens, a good sign that they are learning from our mistakes. These are our kids, the ones who have watched us share their baby photos and our conference dance pictures. They are online natives who want to keep their lives more private now that they are in control. The younger generation is learning that what you say online can be held against you, affecting jobs and relationships future and current.

[3] Source: http://bit.ly/TeenPrivacy

60

Social Media Success Is None of Your Brand's Business

WHEN IT COMES to the concept of *UnSelling* and social media, the key is to remember that the best way to have your product, service, or content spread is by creating amazing products, service, or content. We go to social media for selfish purposes—because our friends are there, to watch funny videos, and to share our lives online. We don't go there for commercials.

The thing is, no one really wants to be social with their watches, jeans, or toilet paper.

We fell in love with social because it created communities for us around the world. We could stay in touch with friends we never got to see anymore and share the day-to-day stuff that make us all human. Brands were sold on the idea of being part of social media because we were all there, and they treated social as they would commercial space on our favorite TV shows. Brands set up shop, pushed out their messages, and waited for the windfall to hit.

The problem is that no matter how many search engine optimization (SEO) tricks they played or money they paid, we just kept finding ways to ignore them. The companies that did cool, human, actually social things succeeded. Those that thought they could buy or push their way into a spot in our feed had to continue to find new ways to trick us for each and every click.

When we love products or have great experiences, we share them with other people. We tell stories. Social media didn't create this; we used to use cave walls and parchment and books. We even use to tell one another face to face! We are drawn to products with stories of their own and choose the things that fit in with the one we are telling of ourselves. Just look at Nike or Apple and how those companies communicate. What does being their customer say about you? People talk about products like those whether the company is present or not, because their fans are ecstatic fans, and they are part of a community of people who love their products.

Social media success is none of a brand's business. The future of social won't be about more and more paid spots or keywords; the future of social will be brands saying, "We are just going to focus on being the best we can be and let you do the talking." Social media will become a place brands go to listen, to answer questions when asked, to return the high five when fans say hi. And they will leave the rest of the talking to us.

61

Conclusion

THROUGHOUT *UNSELLING* WE'VE been talking about changing our focus in business, stepping away from the funnel vision that's keeping us from succeeding in today's online world. We learned about pulse and pivot: how making the most of each and every point of contact with our customers creates social success for our businesses and that understanding pulse is our best marketing, filling the sales cloud with the kinds of impressions we could never push out using traditional publicity. We looked at industries that have changed and how the most successful companies navigated through by checking their own pulse and the pulse of their customers. And last, we looked at the tools you can use to make *UnSelling* happen for your business.

One person, one interaction, can make and shape a brand, from a well-known giant, multinational chain to the corner store. This creates a tremendous opportunity for individuals to make a difference at work and feel of value each and every day. No matter what your job is, whether you are a business owner just getting started or an employee at a company you love, your passion and expertise make all the difference. Branding isn't a logo; branding is the impression we leave on people.

Businesses can no longer sit back and assume they know more than their customers. Today, the power of information has shifted.

Purchase decisions are made before the pitch and outside your funnel. An educated market with a voice demands more. We are connected online to a world of opinions and reviews, a great collaborative conversation we trust, much more than any ad campaign. Consumer choice is the enemy of company complacency.

Valuing people is at the heart of *UnSelling*. Treating our employees, vendors, and customers well is the start of creating amazing experiences and standing out in today's busy world of information and reviews. Hire for passion. Create quality products, service, and content worth sharing. Make it easy for fans to tell your story for you. Facilitate community around your product or service. That is the way to create an ecstatic customer base. That's *UnSelling*.

Thank you so much for taking the time to read *UnSelling*. If you enjoyed it, we wrote a bunch of other books you could check out, too!

- *UnMarketing. Stop Marketing, Start Engaging.* This is the book that started it all. If you're ready to stop ineffective marketing and put building relationships with customers first, this is the book to get you on the right track. A great resource for companies of all sizes and a guide for business students around the world.
- *The Book of Business Awesome/The Book of Business UnAwesome.* The first and only business flip-book you'll ever need! On one side, we look at the amazing stories in business and learn how engaging your customers and employees can make your company thrive. On the other side, we learn what not to do: the cost of not listening, engaging, or being great at what you do.
- *QR Codes Kill Kittens.* A picture book for those who are fed up. Learn how to alienate customers, dishearten employees, and drive our business into the ground. A collection of hilarious, real-life examples from marketing, branding, networking, public relations, and customer service all to show you what you shouldn't be doing in business.

Come join Alison and me at the UnPodcast.com, where we talk about the week's brand blunders and train wrecks, send climbers up Moron Mountain, and even share the occasional good story or two. You can watch the show or download the podcast to your favorite podcast app.

If you'd like to learn more about having me speak at your event, visit my speaker page ScottStratten.com. To learn more or sign up for my newsletter, where I share blog posts only when I have something awesome to say, visit UnMarketing.com. I love hearing from readers and learning more about them. If you have business stories to share or just want to say hi, you can reach me on Twitter @UnMarketing and Alison @UnAlison; Facebook at www.Facebook.com/UnMarketing; e-mail at Scott@Un-Marketing.com and Alison at Alison@Un-Marketing.com. Hopefully you haven't flatlined on us.

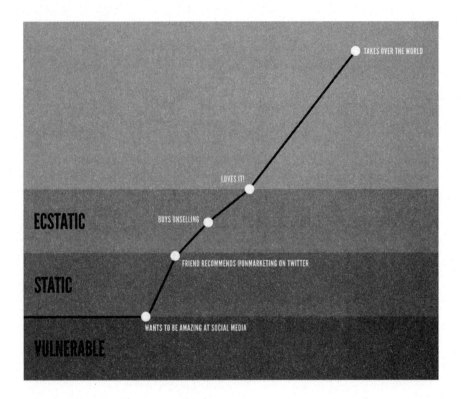

Index